The Graphic Designer's Electronic-Media Manual

© 2012 Rockport Publishers

First published in the United States of America in 2012 by
Rockport Publishers, a member of Quayside Publishing Group

....

100 Cummings Center
Suite 406-L
Beverly, Massachusetts 01915-6101
Telephone: (978) 282-9590
Fax: (978) 283-2742
www.rockpub.com

....

Visit rockpaperink.com to share your opinions, creations, and passion for design.

10 9 8 7 6 5 4 3 2 1

ISBN: 978-1-59253-778-5

Digital edition published in 2012
eISBN: 978-1-61058-401-2

Library of Congress Cataloging-in-Publication Data
Tselentis, Jason.
The graphic designer's electronic-media manual : how to apply visual
design principles to engage users on desktop, tablet, and mobile websites
/ Jason Tselentis.
        p. cm.
Includes bibliographical references and index.
ISBN 978-1-59253-778-5 -- ISBN 1-59253-778-2 -- ISBN 978-1-61058-
401-2 (digital ed.)
1. Graphic design (Typography) 2. Information display systems. I. Title. II.
Title: How to apply visual design principles to engage users on desktop,
tablet, and mobile websites.
Z246.T84 2012
686.2'2–dc23

                                    2011043772

Design: Jason Tselentis

Printed in China

Dedicated to HEATHER TSELENTIS

Interns: Mitchell Phillips & Aaron Rich

Special Thanks: David Barringer, G. David Brown, Gerry Derksen, Chad Dresbach,
Tom Garner, Bryony Gomez-Palacio, Steven Heller, Natalia Ilyin, Eric Karjaluoto,
Tamara LaValla, Tan Le, Zan Maddox, Dorothy Ostrowski, James Sack, Jason Santa Maria,
Rishi Sodha, David Stokes, Ben Visser, Armin Vit, Ellen Ward, and Anton Webb

Jason Tselentis

The Graphic Designer's Electronic-Media Manual

How to apply visual design principles to engage users on desktop, tablet, and mobile websites

Rockport Publishers
100 Cummings Center, Suite 406L
Beverly, MA 01915

rockpub.com • rockpaperink.com

CONTENTS

Reflections on Electronic Media

When Apple delivered the first LaserWriter with PostScript printing in 1985, few designers leapt at the opportunity to learn the PostScript language. Despite the fact that PostScript enabled laser printers to output high-resolution graphics instead of the dot-matrix prints many computer users were accustomed to, nobody felt that learning PostScript would give them a competitive or creative advantage. Designers were busy enough trying to understand how to operate the other revolutionary tool at their disposal: the desktop computer. And with the Macintosh, the days of learning languages, programming, or commands in order to get the computer to do what you wanted seemed like a thing of the past. You just had to point and click.

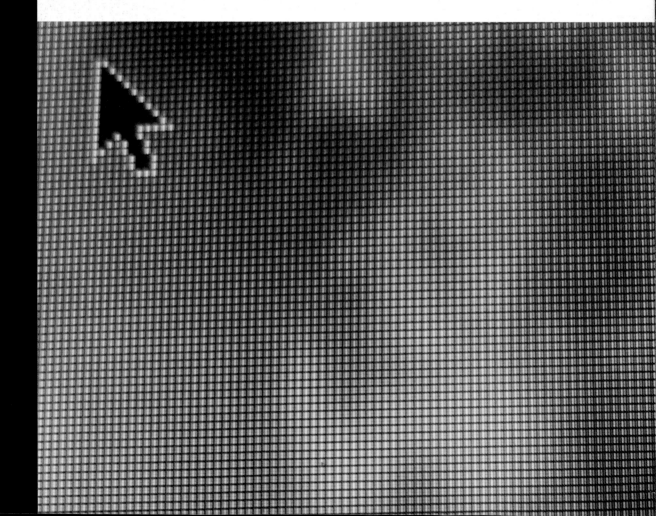

Ten years later, the Internet began to grab hold of computer users, and with the Internet came the promise of a new communication platform: the web. Text and graphics could be transmitted via digital communication, without the need for printing or, for that matter, PostScript. Instead, HTML became the de facto method of designing information in a presentable way for web browsers such as Mosaic, Netscape, and AOL. Mathematicians were some of the first experts to master HTML, especially since early iterations of the markup had a mathematical foundation. Computer scientists and engineers later adopted HTML, and experts from the World Wide Web Consortium (W3C) helped HTML move past the math and into the markup we know today.

As with PostScript, few designers took on the heavy lifting of learning HTML through the late 1990s, especially when software such as Adobe's PageMill and Gonet's GoLive (which became an Adobe property in 1999) allowed the same drag-and-drop functionality that so many designers had become accustomed to with software such as Illustrator, PageMaker, QuarkXPress, and FreeHand. With PageMill and GoLive, designers could easily place text, drag images onto a stage, and create links to other content areas. Customizing typography happened with the click of a button and selection of a color swatch from a toolbar. But at the same time, designers began to see the limitations of HTML, especially when tools such as Macromedia Flash could help them build slick websites with fonts outside of standards such as Arial, Georgia, Times, and Verdana. And animating images and typography could easily happen thanks to another set of clicks, drags, and drops.

While the aforementioned designers took on the task of learning and producing websites on their own with software and without writing much code, others came to appreciate outsourcing production to expert developers. And in doing so, they could assure themselves, and their clients, that the website would operate as needed. Now the designer could focus on the user interface—the graphics and visual communication—and leave the backend programming and development to another party. But, by outsourcing the backend development, it cost them revenue—the design firms and creative agencies had to give up weighty fees to outside vendors that they themselves could have charged and could have kept in-house. While not *the* factor, this lost revenue was in fact one of the reasons many became designers/developers: creators of the graphic and visual communication (the frontend) and programmers of the inner workings necessary to make the website function (the backend).

For designers today, the web pervades our lives. Should all designers understand and be able to design for the web? Not necessarily. Print-only opportunities exist. But if you take a look at today's job openings, you'll notice that a majority of them require some knowledge of web design, user interface design, as well as HTML and CSS. Knowing popular Content Management Systems (CMSes) such as WordPress and Drupal helps too. One of the biggest arguments made against taking on web design jobs has been "I already have to know about Adobe software, and layout, fonts, and color theory. If I have to know about one more thing, then that job isn't for me." Not necessarily. In a market where millions of designers are all competing for the same slice of the pie, knowing a little bit extra goes a long way.

Designers have always had to learn a little bit extra. So learning one more tool, medium, or piece of software should come easily. And not to oversimplify things, but designing for the web calls upon many of the same principles designers learned for the printed page. Granted, the format is different: Instead of the flat, static surface, you now have a screen. And, yes, screen sizes can change: There are small, medium, large, and even extra-large screens such as widescreen televisions. The color spaces are different: Print is subtractive (CMYK) and digital is additive (RGB). Technical matters aside, the print realm—like the electronic one—is built of type and image. For the web design neophyte, thinking along those lines not only makes the task of designing for the web manageable, but it also keeps things fundamental. And if there's one thing that designers need to be more conscious of, it's the fact that the fundamentals they possess are, in fact, transferable. Being able to solve problems across the range of print, digital, and/or environmental media has been, and always will be, our strong suit.

TERMINOLOGY

Designers + Producers

Experience Designer: In the late 1990s and early 2000s, graphic designers, interactive designers, environmental designers, and packaging designers, among others, began referring to themselves in this manner to highlight how users interact with their designs. This job title continues to be used in general terms, and goes beyond media and tools.

Developer (also called Programmer): This person creates the backend that makes a frontend design function or animate for the user.

Interactive Designer: Generally speaking, all designers are interactive designers since users work with and interface with the objects they make. However, an interactive designer focuses on not only the user interface, but also the human computer interaction, and may have a strong background in heuristics or psychology and cognitive science.

Producer: This person works on or oversees all aspects of electronic-media creation. Producers may be experts in a single design area, but they could also have a journeyman's knowledge of how each designer must contribute to the project. This can be a management position or a hands-on creative one, or both.

Traditional Designer (also called Graphic Designer, Conventional Designer): These are the designers who take on projects that use printed media as the output. The title may also refer to designers who work on projects that are not digital in nature.

Web Designer: These designers develop websites for desktop computers, tablets such as the iPad, and smaller mobile devices such as phones.

Production

Backend (or Back End, also called Programming, Development, Production): This refers to the code, instructions, controls, and/or operations that happen behind the frontend; often invisible to the end-user, who interfaces with the media. Programmers specialize in this area of production; however, other designers have also been known to do this work.

Frontend (or Front End, also called Interface Design, User Interface Design): This refers to the text, colors, buttons, imagery, animation, movies, menus, and/or interactivity a user interfaces with when viewing electronic media on his computer, tablet, or handheld device. Designers will create the frontend using a range of software; however, graphic designers have been known to design these interfaces without doing any of the backend whatsoever.

Look and Feel (also called Aesthetic, Style, Appearance): This refers to the way a website appears to match (or not match) its content, theme, or brand needs. Graphic elements such as color, image, type choice, and composition will add up to build an appropriate concept that is less about decoration and more about form and function.

Research/Testing

Heuristics: This is the science behind user testing that evaluates a design's successes and failures. This diverse practice uses a number of metrics to assess electronic media such as websites, computer software, and digital kiosks.

Wireframe (or Wire Frame, also called Box Model or Prototype): This describes a loose, sketch-based website that shows the relationship between the visual content and the format in which it will be displayed. Wireframes are intended for preliminary design reviews and testing to identify any visual problems before the full frontend gets designed. These can be interactive, built for clicking, navigating, and animating, but they can also be built-in software such as Illustrator for static viewing on-screen or in print.

Twelve Fundamentals

A surprising number of graphic designers avoid designing for the web because they fear the production and programming work (the backend). This happens because they think too far ahead, something designers do very well in most cases, in order to understand the short- and long-term issues related to problem solving. A designer will likely look forward to producing the website, and all the technical things that go into that construction. Instinctively, designers consider who will take on the difficult task of doing the backend development and programming. Next, they'll think about what limitations that process may put on their creative direction. A vicious cycle happens where the designer goes back and forth between *I don't understand what goes into a web design project on the backend* and *Since I don't know that backend, there's no way for me to know how to do the frontend design correctly.* In the end, the designer will give up on the idea of taking on said project because he cannot address either of those issues.

While designers may not have the programming acumen to develop and produce the website, they do possess the visual literacy necessary to lay out a website, and calling upon these fundamentals serves as the first step in taking on a web design problem. The twelve fundamentals that follow are neither a comprehensive list nor a formula for success. They are more descriptive than prescriptive, and are intended to show designers how some of the visual principles they already know can be applied to web design.

1 *Know the Material*

By reading the content, a designer takes the first step toward developing a concept, a key ingredient in successfully solving any visual problem. Whether you're designing a large-scale enterprise site with a massive amount of content or a microsite with a minimum amount, you should read and analyze all of the material that could, should, or will go into the site design. Researching outside and in addition to the given material is also worthwhile, and is not limited to market-related materials, brand positioning, trend analysis, and media use. Consider a full SWOT (Strengths, Weaknesses, Opportunities, Threats) analysis to fully plan and evaluate the job.

By specializing in marketing and design for the sports, hospitality, and entertainment industries, carbonhouse understands how to create engaging visual communications for venues such as the Memphis Orpheum Theatre and Cleveland PlayhouseSquare.

2 *Know the Audience*

Designers have always had to understand the audience and how they will engage with the material. Understanding consumer behavior, brand loyalty, reading habits, learning styles, and the bevy of factors that play into those issues and influences are just some of the ways that designers can begin to define users' anthropological makeup.

If given the choice between a text-heavy website with static photographs and an interactive online game, most Red Bull drinkers would opt for the latter. Archrival understood this, and developed an entertaining online game that pulled consumers closer to the brand. For the Travis Pastrana Super Mega Nitro Jump game, Archrival put users into the action of riding a dirt bike, speedboat, donkey, magic carpet, golf cart, and even more ridiculous vehicles.

Understand the Scope

Ask a number of questions at the outset in order to determine project control, implementation, and finalization. How much work needs to be done? What amount of text and imagery will go into the design? Who supplies that material? Where will it all reside? What updates, if any, will need to be made over time? And what about a timeline, and any foreseeable delays? Throughout this analysis, keep quality in mind, along with the team makeup and creative process that ensures it. And be wary of people adding things to an already-defined project that will create what's known as scope creep.

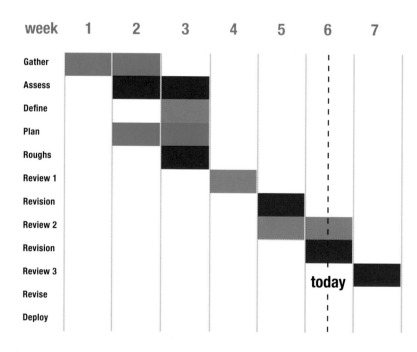

Gantt charts assign tasks to days, or in this case weeks, to give a visualization of the project components. Steps can include gathering, discovery, problem understanding, calendar definition, team building, design, revisions, and final outcome. Certain tasks can get color coded and assigned to teams, and critical tasks may receive hot colors such as red or orange. Tasks may push forward or backward to adjust for internal and external factors. In some cases, the final outcome isn't always foreseeable.

4

Understand the Final Production

Traditional designers who work predominantly in printed media know the specifics of building a document that's press-ready, specifying the right paper, getting bids on a job, and seeing the design through the printing and delivery process. Electronic media has its own final production process with checkpoints in place to meet the end goal and quality concerns. The five key checkpoints, in addition to visual design, include implementation, testing, documentation, launch, and maintenance. During implementation, developers program the site so that it functions. Testing investigates how the site operates on browsers and the ways users interact with it. Documentation collects all of that information and analyzes it in order to aid in the launch and maintenance. Finally, designers may have to come to grips with the word final, as Eric Karjaluoto explains: "Designers have to become more accustomed to the notion of defined job 'cutoffs.' When a print job goes to press the changes end; on a website they seemingly never have to. As such, designers have to clearly note when the scope of a project has come to a close, and address additional content changes and software/media upgrades as separate (billable) projects."

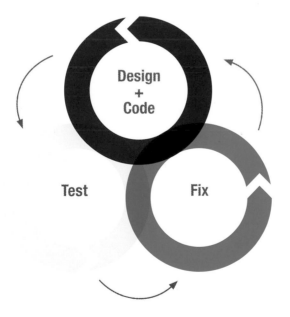

Design, development, and release can lead to ongoing coding, and fixing. These iterative and overlapping steps may happen repeatedly because of fluctuating user needs, text or image content, and hardware or software changes.

Designer Christian Helms and developer David Guillory built the Austin Beerworks product browser using an unconventional horizontal scrolling mechanism that keeps all of the content above the fold.

The Fold

5

Print designers had used the term "above the fold" to reference where the feature story or photography sat on a folded newspaper's cover. Web designers adapted this term for their own needs, since web browsers have a similar demarcation at the bottom of a screen. Other variants include above the scroll, but the meaning stays the same: Users treat content in a browser's immediate viewable area as the most important material. This topic is still open for debate, especially during a time when screen sizes vary from small (phones) to medium (tablets and laptops) to large (personal computers, and even widescreen televisions).

Users who navigate to the Brewery content will find a longer, portrait-formatted composition that requires them to scroll down to read the brewing information graphic.

Adaptability

One of the more challenging facets of web design has to do with adaptability. Not only do various web browsers exist, but also operating systems and screen sizes vary. And none of this considers user needs and preferences, an altogether different adaptability challenge designers have to face.

Jairo Goldflus's online portfolio, designed by Belmer Negrillo, uses a landscape format to keep all of the content viewable, regardless of the screen size. The composition also ensures that no content goes below the fold.

7 Rough It Out

No matter the project, designers are accustomed to making rough visual layouts before tackling the details with software. Pencil and paper have long been the basis for doing so, and sketching material out allows for quick and easy placement, replacement, and editing. Moreover, you can see the big picture, whereas software often tempts designers into playing with specifics like fonts, colors, and textures, long before arriving at a framework. Once the structure has been built, compose box models using software such as Fireworks or Illustrator to identify specifics such as grid structure and type size. Real-world matters such as typography will also come into play.

Although designer Jason Santa Maria works in the digital domain, creating websites for large-scale clients, he always starts creating in his sketchbook.

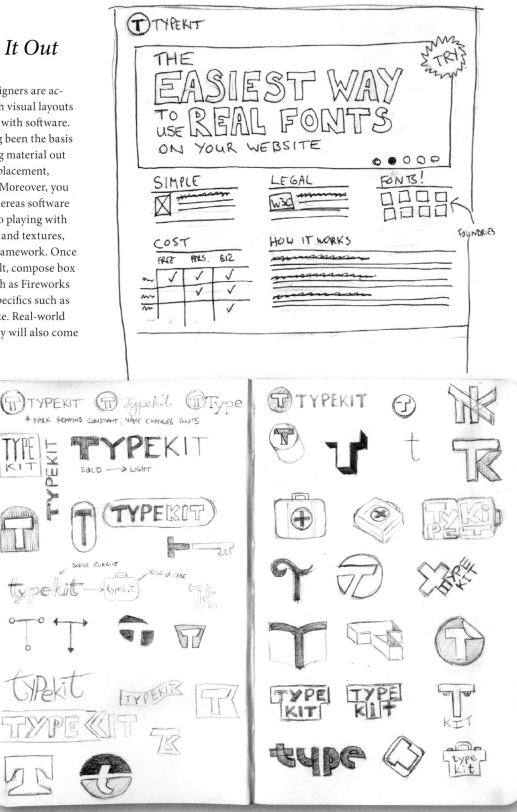

8

It's All Type and Image

Two components that go into most visual communications are typography and image. There are cases where one is used more than the other, or where one is used exclusively, but most of the time they're the key ingredients for composing layouts. Web design neophytes who keep this principle in mind will go a long way toward developing themselves into capable digital designers. But those accustomed to print design have a difficult time understanding how typography functions on the web, especially when dealing with size. Print designers will typically set type anywhere from 8 to 9 points for book text, sometimes going as large as 12 points. Subheads and headlines appear in 14 points or larger. But long bodies of text type on the web will be as small as 14 points, and as large as 16, with headlines and subheads appearing as large as 26 points. While these rules aren't set in stone, the point is that digital type benefits from larger sizes than most traditional designers are used to setting.

Mandy Brown uses large type that's easy on the eyes at her website, A Working Library. Other niceties, such as drop caps and paragraph indentions, bring print conventions to the web, making for an engaging experience.

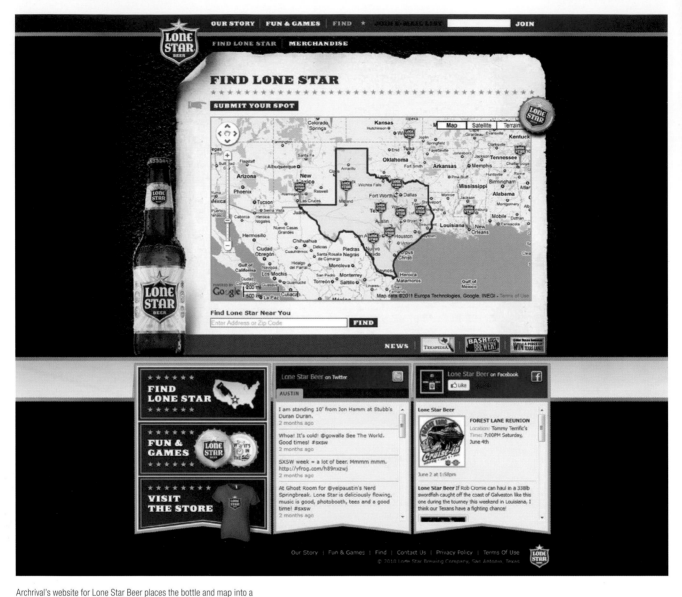

Archrival's website for Lone Star Beer places the bottle and map into a large content area to feature the product, and then situates secondary content beneath it in a three-column fashion.

Use a Grid

Should you always use a grid when designing for the web? Perhaps not. But inspect the sites you visit on a daily basis. In all likelihood, they all use a grid. Grids used for digital devices may be fixed, variable, or a combination of the two. In each case, columns delineate vertical zones and flowlines delineate horizontal ones. Additionally, a baseline grid may exist to align content from one column to the next. Distinct content areas within these grids have also been known as divs, referring to the HTML element.

10

Contrast, Contrast, Contrast

Contrast happens when noticeable differences happen between one item and another, such as foreground and background, headline and body text, and one content area and another. Typography should be significantly darker compared to its background tone. A feature image should be larger than a secondary or tertiary image in order to get the attention it deserves.

Differences in type size and image placement help users find information at the University of Texas at Austin's Visitor Center website. Color-coding content, such as having the Campus area tan and the Faculty area purple, further aids users in navigating the content. Lastly, Fangman Design placed the typography over darker-toned photos to ensure legibility for the reader.

11 Interface Unity

Designers who take on the lofty task of creating their own online presence should instinctively create a unified identity, where every facet of the interface looks the same from one content area to the next. A unified online presence has become more important during a time when designers have to maintain not only their own online portfolio, but also their weblog, online shopping portal, or other ventures such as a Twitter stream. Using the same font family, color palette, grid structure, and logo/wordmark will go a long way toward projecting a consistent and well-designed image.

Letterer, illustrator, and designer Jessica Hische composed her online weblog and store with a uniform visual scheme that gives users a predictable experience across these and other levels of her website.

12

Interface Variety

Having a unified interface look does not mean that it should have a singular aesthetic, with fonts and images lacking variation in size or placement. Most websites have a wealth of content, and designers need to create a sense of hierarchy so that the user knows what is important, where to look first, and how to find more information. Be sure to design an interface with enough visual differentiation to support the content, theme, and concept while also meeting the needs of the client and user.

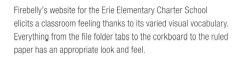

Firebelly's website for the Erie Elementary Charter School elicits a classroom feeling thanks to its varied visual vocabulary. Everything from the file folder tabs to the corkboard to the ruled paper has an appropriate look and feel.

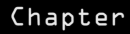

Chapter 1 THE

DIGITAL REALITY

The story of the graphic and advertising profession in the age that governs our lives, producing sounds, colors

The Online Experience

THE INTERFACE ▪ Prior to the graphical user interface (GUI, pronounced "gooey") the only way we could get data from a computer was through the command-line interface, a method still available on most operating systems. But today we use a keyboard, mouse, trackpad, or touchscreen to click, drag, and select icons, buttons, imagery, and text. Many of our modern-day technologies have a user interface of some kind: microwaves, televisions, mobile phones, and even refrigerators. They may have metaphorical buttons like folders on our computer desktops, or text-labeled buttons like those on our microwave.

But how are web-based user interfaces (WUIs) different? The short answer is that they aren't: In each case, the interface acts as a device for us to achieve something. On the web, an interface may help us find a piece of information, like a book in an online catalog. A search form would enable us to type in a title, author name, keyword, subject, ISBN, or a combination of the above to complete that search. Other sites may have the express purpose of delivering content for us to read, and the site could show us what news is important, or it could deliver it according to personal preferences and ranking we have saved on the site.

Personal preferences are one of the key ways that WUIs differ from printed media. With a printed newspaper, you get the news on the front page, set in the paper's established typeface and type size. But viewing that same news company's site online would enable you to customize the typeface and type size to suit your needs and preferences. Depth also factors into an online experience, as well as the WUI. While information may get displayed in chunks and have an essential hierarchy, in many cases we can dig deeper to get more information about the material at hand. Finding, reading, learning, shopping, and comparing are not static happenings, but rather dynamic and deep occurrences.

The Weddings Unveiled website designed by Joshua Mauldin lets users read the magazine using a web browser, and advance pages forward or rewind them backward using arrow keys that many of us are familiar with. Those who wish to see the entire publication in thumbnails can click the 3 × 3 grid button to do so.

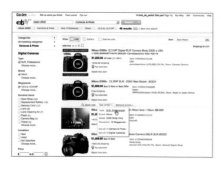

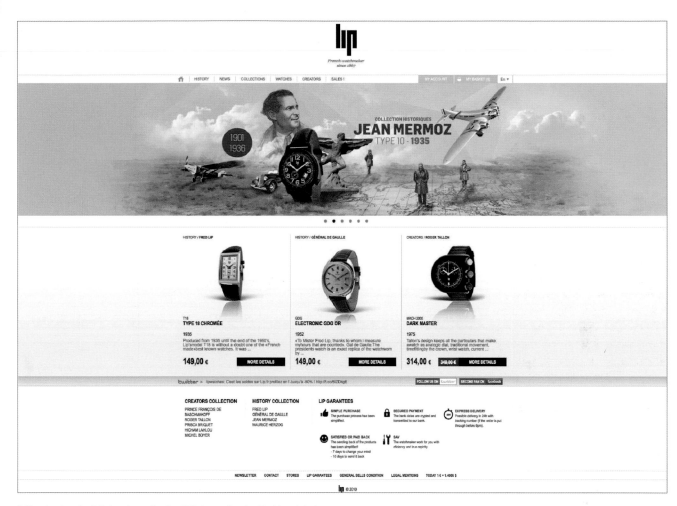

Unlike printed media, digital media can flow in a 360-degree direction. The Lip website by Ultranoir lets users navigate content left and right, such as the primary image header featuring Jean Mermoz. But you can also dig deeper to learn about products by clicking on links.

By installing some of the features available at the Garden by eBay, users can have a richer online shopping experience that lets them multitask, save searches, and dig for more information. Belmer Negrillo developed extended search results to give details about products, such as this Nikon camera, with mouseovers and clicks. As an added bonus, a list of saved, and albeit unrelated products, appears at the website's footer with expanded viewing.

INPUT AND OUTPUT ▪ We interact with computers using a distinct set of hardware tools, including, but not limited to, the keyboard, mouse, and touchscreen. Through each device, a user will input a set of commands in order to achieve an intended purpose. We type on keyboards, using numbers, lowercase letters, and uppercase letters. Through a mouse, we point, click, and click and drag. Touchscreen enables a number of finger- and hand-based gestures such as tapping, pinching, dragging, swiping, and wiping with one finger or many fingers.

Computers accept our input and deliver content through digital displays and video projectors, as well as printers. Computer displays have enclosed electronic circuitry, the first of which were cathode ray tubes (CRTs), until they were replaced by liquid crystal displays (LCDs). Projectors receive video signals and transform them into imagery onto a larger surface such as a wall or projector screen.

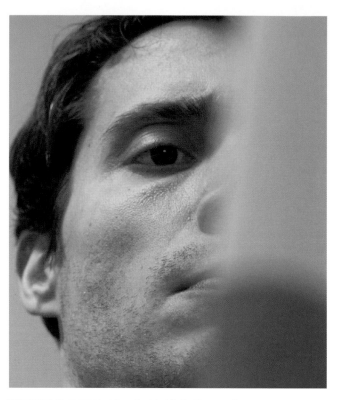

With print media, people can enlarge items by bringing the paper closer.

Handheld devices will often give users the opportunity to bring the media closer for viewing. In some cases, we can even make the display larger to view details.

We now have the ability to input with a mouse, trackpad, keyboard, or touchscreen. Cameras and microphones also accept user input.

TYPES OF EXPERIENCES ■ When we go online, each of us has a different purpose in mind. Sometimes we want entertainment, other times we want to learn something, or perhaps we want to share with our close friends and relatives. This experience has broadened and changed dramatically over the past decade, and will continue to expand. But ultimately, we all share one thing: the online quest itself. We encounter educational, commercial, entertainment, and networking websites. Those categories may overlap in any number of ways, such that an entertaining game may bring us closer to a product, in an effort to make us more aware of a brand. A game may also be developed around an existing brand to help foster interest in the brand, thereby moving us to purchase related products. In each case, the experience must be engaging. But what defines an engaging experience? Engagement often deals with surface properties, such as aesthetics, or what has become known as look and feel.

Look and feel is how a website appears using graphic elements such as color, image, typography, and composition to build an information design or visual concept. An engaging online news website would likely look and feel like its printed counterpart, with feature material above the fold and secondary content appearing smaller or below the fold. No matter the website, engagement is closely related to appropriateness, where the visual design matches the content and delivers the best end product for the user. James Sack, creative director at carbonhouse, explains, "A memorable experience at a theater doesn't begin in the lobby. It starts online. We want to create a seamless experience with our client's brand for each visitor. Many of our typography choices are used to give a consistent feel for patrons or concertgoers. We pull design elements from the physical venues into the site's overall look. So really our typography process starts during our initial client visit, well before the design stage."

An entertainment venue such as the XL Center in Hartford, Connecticut, incorporates graphic elements from the facility into the website, and by designing the website in this way, carbonhouse links the physical brand with the online one.

The University of Texas at Austin's Virtual Visitor Center teaches people all about the campus and school life. As this is an educational site, Fangman Design created distinct portals to teach people about student life, faculty, the campus, and quick facts.

Archrival developed the Colt 45 Ink the Can site so that users could enter a design for a 16 oz. (473 ml) Colt 45 can. Not only did the site let users submit designs, but it also showcased all entries, and allowed visitors to vote and comment on each of them. Sites like these create brand engagement by involving the consumer with the product and also foster socialization among product loyalists.

Website Types

Public Service: humanitarian causes, such as those related to health, wellness, safety, or utility

Institutional: a site delivering material about a religious, educational, or social organization

Government: information about national, state, or community controls, regulations, personnel, or administration

Educational: has the express purpose of delivering information, from which a user will learn something

Reference: an information repository with a range of media

Editorial: news, commentary, and/or criticism, akin to newspapers or magazines

Entertainment: text, image, video, or a combination intended to arouse enjoyment or emotion

Experimental: usually defined by the creator or the media, but oftentimes radically new in its delivery or style

Gaming: sites for play or sport, where people compete for an intended purpose or prize

Blog: a site built upon a system of entries that may be sorted and viewed by subject or tag; authors range from subject matter experts to hobbyists to casual observers

Sharing: text, image, or video sites that enable uploading and viewing of said content

Communities: places where people can come together and form tribes to share information about themselves or their happenings; may be closed, by invitation only, or open to any user

Social Networking: a community-based site, with the express purpose of exploring communities and sharing information

Promotion: a site that can further a cause, person, product, place, or purpose, such as a site to spread the word about a presidential candidate or a site that encourages people to visit Spain in the summer

Commercial and Transactional: a site that sells goods, services, or activities, enabling people to view, sort, choose, and purchase said item all from the Internet

Customer Service: attempts to fulfill the needs, questions, curiosities, or problems a consumer will have

Employment and Careers: for finding or placing jobs, as well as developing one's own career using online tools and resources

Intranet: a closed and private system that delivers information only for members of an organization, typically over a secure network not accessible to outsiders

Users

PARTICIPATION ▪ Site visitors may interact with content in a number of ways. They can select information, move through content, enter information, share content, or alter the interface. Not every site will allow a user to complete these actions, but at the most basic level a site should enable users to visit, view, and move through information using an input device. More complex sites invite users to enter information, comments, or reviews, so they can build and expand the website. Allowing them to share content by uploading imagery or video is just another way of turning users into active, online participants.

This is a key difference between online media and printed media: participation. The term web 2.0 has been used to refer to the dawn of a participatory Internet, and is closely associated with Tim O'Reilly and the O'Reilly Media Web 2.0 conference held in 2004. Web 1.0, on the other hand, was more about the user retrieving and receiving information rather than building and adding it to the Internet. Cooperation, crowd-sourcing, blogging, and rich experiences have become synonymous with web 2.0. But it's the rich experiences that mean the most to graphic designers, who can now seize the opportunity to create engaging interfaces because of high-performing computers, web browsers, and Internet connections. Eric Karjaluoto, creative director at smashLAB, sums it up by saying, "This new-ish space allows designers to do some interesting, challenging, and rewarding work. Better yet, good designers will find that the same critical thinking that helped them create effective printed work is just as important when designing for screens."

Belmer Negrillo's design for the Vuvox website lets users create interactive slideshows and presentations using content they keep at a number of online photo-sharing sites, including Flickr, Picasa Albums, YouTube, and Facebook. The Creation gateway lets users pick one of three tools to do so.

In addition to creating media in your web browser at the Vuvox site, you can also browse media in the site's Explore browsing tool.

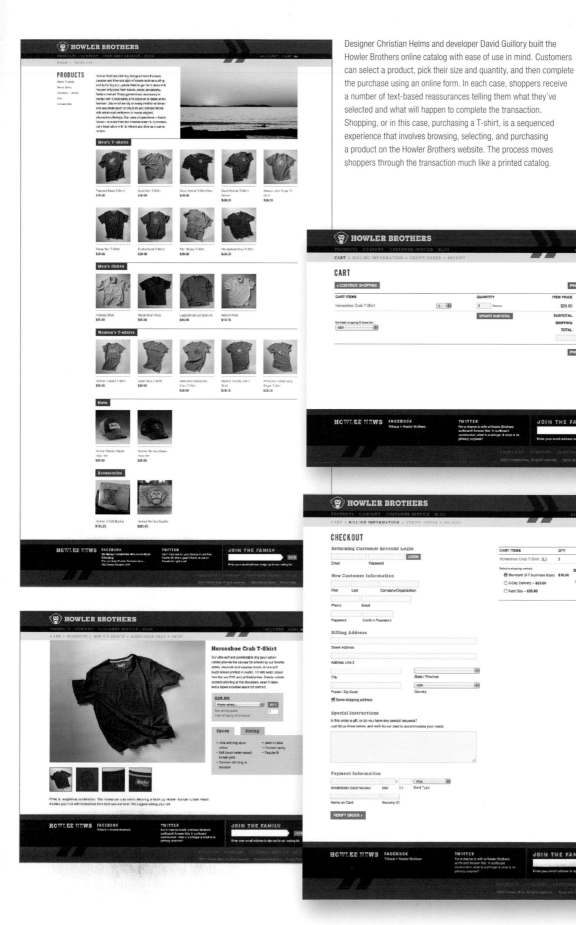

Designer Christian Helms and developer David Guillory built the Howler Brothers online catalog with ease of use in mind. Customers can select a product, pick their size and quantity, and then complete the purchase using an online form. In each case, shoppers receive a number of text-based reassurances telling them what they've selected and what will happen to complete the transaction. Shopping, or in this case, purchasing a T-shirt, is a sequenced experience that involves browsing, selecting, and purchasing a product on the Howler Brothers website. The process moves shoppers through the transaction much like a printed catalog.

USER PERSONAS ▪ Culture, age, education, gender, ethnicity, employment, social interaction, health, and income are just some of the factors that contribute to an individual's personality and online persona. Understanding user personas is akin to understanding any audience, where enough preliminary data gets analyzed to create a picture of who will use the design. A number of methods exist to help collect this information, some of which include online or print-based surveys, role playing, interviews, and sourcing from existing results. Surveys, role playing, and interviews will take more time than sourcing from existing results; however, accessing existing research can cost time and money.

Questions to Help Define the Persona

Will the users be male or female?

How old are they, and what stage are they in their life?

What kind of education do they have?

What are their interests?

Do they have a lot of experience with the Internet?

What kind of experience do they have with computers?

Where will they use the site?

How will they use the site, specifically, on what kind of device?

What are some of the sites they visit on a daily or hourly basis?

What sites do they most enjoy visiting, and why?

Online forms, such as the one designed by Joshua Mauldin for the Azrotech website, are just one way to collect information about people who will view or are viewing a website.

Type	Fearful	Uncertain	Beginner	Intermediate	Advanced	Stumbles a lot	Stumbles	Stumbles a little
Luddite	•	•	•			•		
Neophyte		•	•			•		
Basic			•	•			•	
Power				•	•			•
Programmer					•			•

Luddite: unlearned and, in many cases, skeptical about and opposed to not only the Internet, but new technology in general

Neophyte: has a minimal amount of experience, and may stumble a lot along the way

Basic: knows all about the basics, but may not take the time to learn about cutting-edge or next-generation technology and tools; has developed his own habits that let him complete given tasks in his own way

Power (or Super): has developed his own habits of navigating the Internet, but may also know about alternative or lesser-used methods; mindful of new or cutting-edge technologies and tools; interested in how sites work, but not always capable of completing the backend work to do so

Programmer: will possess many of the attributes of a power user; however, is capable of creating the backend necessary for the site to function

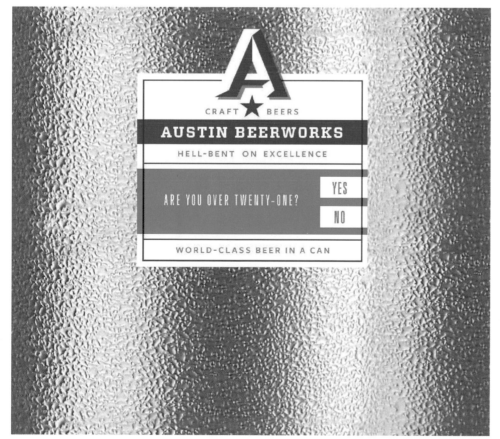

Christian Helms included a gateway at the Austin Beerworks website that asks if users are twenty-one years of age or older. Screening users in this way meets a requirement that some countries have, and also captures data about who has visited the website.

When carbonhouse designed the Alamodome's website, they considered the little details, like making the website's background darker for evening performances. It automatically changes after 6:00 p.m. Central Standard Time. Subtle changes like this connect a site, its content, and the brand itself more directly to people.

Interactivity

A number of conventions exist online, most of which were put in place to aid users: We now have expectations, and a set of givens. Underlines signify links that take us to deeper or different content. Clicking a logo in the topmost menu bar will usually take you back home. A small plus sign on top of an image tells us that clicking it will enlarge the image. Conventions like these are especially helpful for normal users, neophytes, or the rare Luddite who visits a website. But, no matter the user, what things should designers consider as necessities? Eric Karjaluoto, creative director at smashLAB, goes into great detail: "Those 'givens' don't obstruct engagement; in fact, quite the opposite. Interfaces that don't utilize common conventions tend to make people do unnecessary work. Designers sometimes confuse being different with 'engagement.' Aside from the rare exception, this almost always turns out to be a bad thing."

The content itself plays a big role in the engagement, especially when users can connect with it. Karjaluoto continues, "When a site seemingly anticipates my needs and helps me find what I want, I'm satisfied (and maybe even happy). It just goes on from there: Interesting and well-edited stories lead me to care; photos that put me at the heart of the action help me visualize the thing in question; meanwhile, clear and responsive buttons and navigation elements make me feel like I'm in control."

CALENDAR

Join Now : Login

Neighborhood Parents Network

CONNECT · DISCUSS · LEARN · SCHOOL · PARENTPERKS · NEWS · CALENDAR · ABOUT · CONTACT

NPN CALENDAR

	MARCH			APRIL 2011			MAY
	SUN	**MON**	**TUE**	**WED**	**THU**	**FRI**	**SAT**
	27	**28**	**29**	**30**	**31**	**1**	**2**
	Adoption-Play @ Garfield Park Conservatory		Andersonville - Jazzercise @ Beth Emet Synagogue	WMG -TIRED OF FEELING TIRED @ COUNTRY Financial	Elementary School + Parents Dine Out @ Blue Ocean		Andersonville - Story Time @ Flourish Studios
	Single Parents-Puppet Show Storytime @ OpenBooks			Dads n' Beans @ Little Beans			Community Baby Shower - Birth, Baby & Beyond @ Prentice
	3	**4**	**5**	**6**	**7**	**8**	**9**
		CLOSED! NMG-Working Moms Weekday Group @ Tiffany's House		CLOSED! NMG-Stay at Home Moms Group @ Beth's House	WMG Moms of Preschoolers & Up Lunch @ Med Kitchen		Single Parents Easter Egg Coloring and Hunt @ Wright Leadership
				West Town - Bilingual Music Time @ Building Blocks Toy Store			Andersonville - Story Time @ Uncommon Ground
	10	**11**	**12**	**13**	**14**	**15**	**16**
	CANCELED - Andersonville - Mom & Tot Scrapbooking @	West Town Play Time @ Kid City	You & Number 2 @ Little Beans Cafe		WMG Moms of Toddlers Lunch @ Med Kitchen		Green Metropolis Fair @ Irish American Heritage Center
	CANCELED - Andersonville - Beginner Scrapbooking	LS/NorthCenter - Parent & Tot Yoga @ Bloom Yoga	Multiples Pajama Party! @ Gymboree				CLOSED! NMG-Weekend Working Moms Group @ Kelley's
	SSP-Concert in the Park @ Indian Boundary Park/Fieldhouse		Special Night Out: LUNAFEST film festival @ The Music Box				Parent U- Kids Health Expo @ Lakeview YMCA
	17	**18**	**19**	**20**	**21**	**22**	**23**
		Andersonville & Lincoln Square- Mom & Tot Yoga @ Bloom Yoga			WMG Moms of Infants Lunch @ Med Kitchen		The Great Cloth Diaper Change @ Bellybum Boutique
		Moms Over 35 Book Club @ Member's Home					
	24	**25**	**26**	**27**	**28**	**29**	**30**
			Attorney Moms Breakfast @ Caffe Baci	Adoption- Parents' Night Out @ Mayan Palace Mexican Cuisine	Elementary School Parents Monthly Dine Out! @ Buona Terra	Near West&South - Lunch @ Jason's Deli	
			Developmental Differences Parent Support Group @		WMG-Beyond Diapers: Best Practices for Potty Training Your Wee One	You & Number 2 @ Little Beans Cafe	
			Lakeview Mom's Night Out @ Wilde Bar & Restaurant		Expecting & New Parents- Financial Planning @		

Advertise · Contact Us · Twitter · Facebook · © 2011 Neighborhood Parents Network

Firebelly's website for the Neighborhood Parents Network includes a thorough calendar, and automatically highlights the current day to tell people what's happening. Simply identifying the 28th as "today's date" saves people valuable time and creates ease of use.

Navigation and Metaphors

Like it or not, designers contribute to the way users access information, navigating them from one content area to the next. Users will still have control over the material they view and interact with, but it is the designer's job to help them get what they need, delivering reassurances along the way. Reassurances are a powerful tool for helping users identify where they are, where they've been, and where they can go. Many online forms use reassurances to show the amount of progress you've made on a form. Reassurances are just one way to deliver feedback to the user, but engagement is what really matters, as Eric Karjaluoto, creative director at smashLAB, suggests: "If you put aside the mechanics of how the thing functions and instead concentrate on what you're trying to convey, you'll have a good start. A website isn't a bunch of links and buttons; it's a platform for experience."

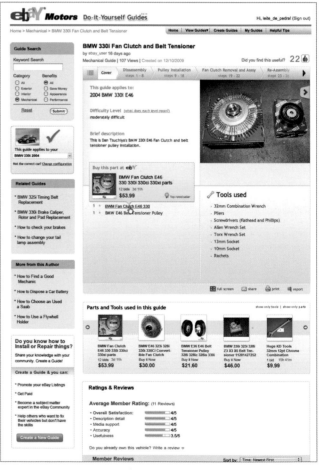

Despite the wealth of information visible at eBay's site, it has continued to be a frequently used tool for shoppers looking for online bargains. Designer Belmer Negrillo made sure to chunk all of the information into quickly digestible bits so that people can see related content, and find what they want on the eBay Motors Do-It-Yourself Guide. Putting the search tool immediately beneath the eBay wordmark helps people inquire about something specific.

FORGE, LLC, formalized a way for people to share a love of good food with the "Eat at FORGE" lunch program. The online reservation system mimics the look of a 1950s diner. Information is collected bit by bit from site visitors, with reassurances given along the way, such as highlighting the choices they've made.

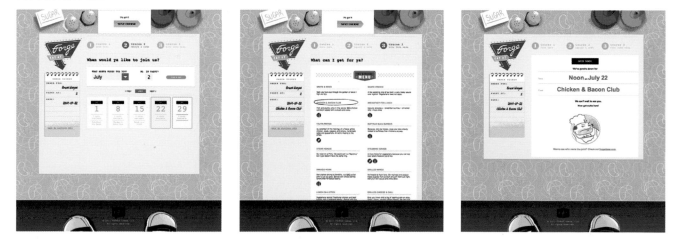

Studiobanks created an unconventional point of view when designing
the blynk organic website. The resultant interface not only takes users
by surprise, but also directly speaks to the natural elements the brand
proudly delivers.

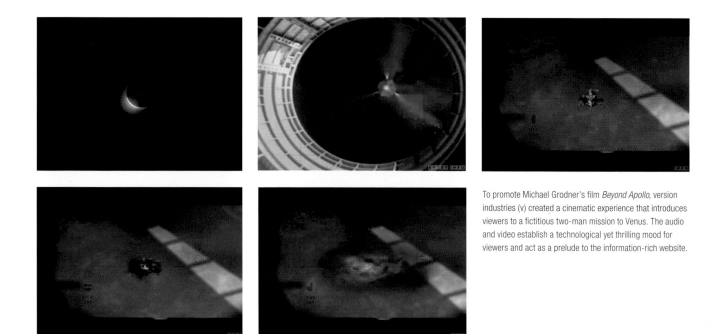

To promote Michael Grodner's film *Beyond Apollo*, version
industries (v) created a cinematic experience that introduces
viewers to a fictitious two-man mission to Venus. The audio
and video establish a technological yet thrilling mood for
viewers and act as a prelude to the information-rich website.

"Engagement on the web has an awful lot to do with telling a good story."
—ERIC KARJALUOTO

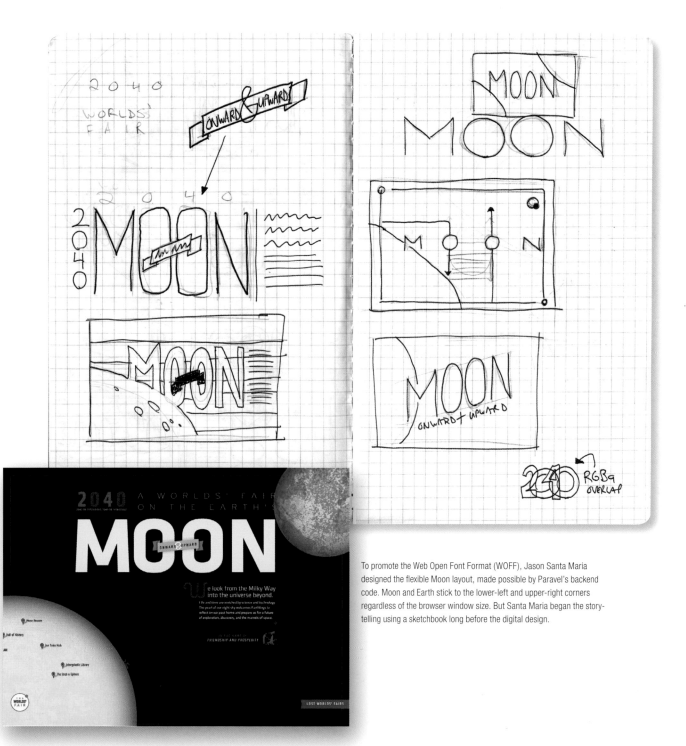

To promote the Web Open Font Format (WOFF), Jason Santa Maria designed the flexible Moon layout, made possible by Paravel's backend code. Moon and Earth stick to the lower-left and upper-right corners regardless of the browser window size. But Santa Maria began the story-telling using a sketchbook long before the digital design.

One of the key ways designers have spurred interaction is through the use of metaphors. On our personal computers, we interact with what has been known as the "desktop." It has a similar look and feel to a physical desktop, insomuch as it contains icons in the shape of folders with a trash can on the Mac OS and a recycling bin on the Windows OS. Much like the desktop metaphor, tabs have become an online metaphor, existing on sites such as Amazon.com and even browsers themselves. For many users, the comfort of having a top-menu tab system persists, and they will oftentimes reference sites as being like Amazon.com simply because of the tab system one site shares with the online retailer.

We recognize tabs from the array of organizational tools we use in the home and office, or kitchen.

Although they do not directly resemble tabs, carbonhouse's design for the Orpheum uses a string of text-based menu items at the top, equipped with a drop-down menu for subnavigation.

Consider how navigation can deliver choices to users, and give them feedback about the choices they make or the ones they have made.

Have active links been highlighted in some way?

What about visited links; is there a way to tell users where they've been?

Can the navigation tell people where they are using color, text, imagery, or a combination?

Can breadcrumbs provide an added reassurance to show people where they started and where they currently reside?

Belmer Negrillo's design for the Vuvox Collage website incorporates a number of tabs on the top menu and secondary content areas such as Hot-spots, Comments/Questions, More by This Author, and Featured.

PRIMARY/SECONDARY NAVIGATION ▪ Menu items will take the place of primary navigation and secondary navigation. The items themselves can appear as text, words, images, or symbols. In the most basic sense, primary navigation will cover a broad content area, such as a button marked "books." Clicking "books" may bring a secondary piece of navigation that displays the genres: fiction, nonfiction, science fiction, fantasy, art, design, photography, or architecture. One of the more common examples of primary and secondary navigation continues to be found at Amazon.com, where its top menu displays the general products or stores and its side menu lets you search deeper within the selected store.

The primary navigation elements about, work, and news appear in these different examples on the right. If a user were to navigate to the about section, he would be taken to a new content area where the secondary navigation elements mission, staff, and location appear. The amount of content or each word's character count will dictate if these or other compositions will work. Simple text-only prototypes such as these help the designer investigate layout opportunities during early client reviews and user testing.

The Hello Poster Show website uses a singular navigation system
at the top, with posters displayed in a gallery style beneath it.

MOVING ▪ Designers have used bursts, bubbles, and banners to get readers' attention for years and these visual devices continue to appear in electronic media. When these devices frustrate users or, worse yet, upset them, the online experience can quickly come to an end. But if attention-getting devices need to announce something new, important, or relevant, it can be done in a way that matches the look and feel, as a temporary or long-term layout.

The Dye Lab's website lets users reposition and even close up-to-date announcements, akin to sticky notes.

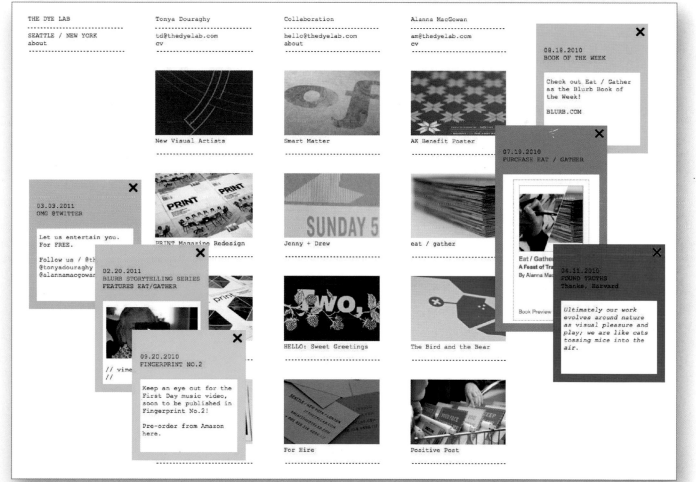

ENABLE SCANNING ▪ Online, people will often do the least amount of work possible. This in no way suggests that people are inherently lazy, but rather that people expect speed and immediacy online. Sites should download quickly. The content needs to be readable without too much of a struggle. And the text should not be too lengthy. What constitutes too lengthy? Lengthy is particularly subjective during a time when many of us read 140-character tweets and 160-character text messages. And sometimes the character counts are well below that. Large amounts of text won't always work online, especially at a landing, or home screen. People expect to see a short and quick overview of everything the site has to offer, or at least some of its highlights. Chunking text content into small and easily digestible bites, placed in modular grid elements, ensures that people will be able to skim over items in a manageable fashion.

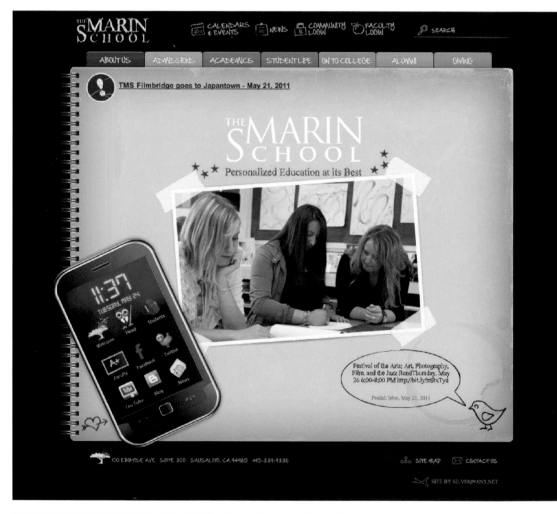

Silverpoint's design for the Marin School uses a home screen with a minimal amount of type, opting to deliver a small graphic in the center with menu items at the top. The small amount of text, relegated to the bottom, is the most recent tweet serving as a short press release about current events.

The David Kirsch Wellness Co. website, designed by Neil Brown, has short introductory sentences under each headline.

At a feature article, the website text amounts to a mere 272 words, approximately one-third the length of a typed, single-spaced letter. But it's the twenty-nine-word (171-character) subhead that tells readers everything they need to know: The Madison Square Club began as a vision. A place where men and women could realize their physical, mental, and spiritual balance in an atmosphere of luxury and serenity.

Making a digital experience easy for users helps them feel comfortable when they interact with the design. This doesn't suggest that the interface or design has to be dumbed down for users, but it should be simple enough for them to enter, experience, and, if warranted, leave. Imagine how difficult it would be for users to find related menu items that were scattered up and down a layout or, worse yet, hidden. Collecting elements into one set of choices gives them a single area to scan and then choose from. If a user gets lost, then an overwhelmed user will certainly get frustrated. Too much content creates a dizzying set of choices, and lengthy content will take up too much time. Condensing menu choices or even an article's lead text will help users quickly get the big picture without taking too much time reading and decoding.

Menu Considerations

Collect: Put related menu choices near one another. They can relate based on subject matter or order of importance.

Condense: Shorten text content, such as menu choices or written lead-in copy, to be only as long as needed. Brevity will encourage scanning so long as it is clear enough to understand.

Cut: Whenever possible, try to remove any loose ends. Removing suffixes such as -ing or -ed can make a lengthy word even a tad shorter, for a quicker read and more layout space.

Twofold Creative designed Coutume Couture's online shopping experience using a less-is-more approach, even going so far as to delineate the steps needed to quickly select clothing, materials, and sizes.

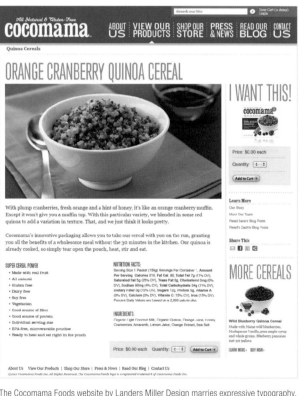

The Cocomama Foods website by Landers Miller Design marries expressive typography, colorful imagery, and well-written copy. The headlines get readers' attention thanks to short and direct statements.

smashLAB positioned small iconography amid OpenRoad's website to deliver cues. The icons enable people to quickly understand what each area of body copy is about.

Chapter **2** MAN
THE

AGING
DESIGN

"*Although graphic design has great power to captivate, persuade, motivate, and delight, it would never get off the ground without effective planning, organization, and management.*"
—TERRY LEE STONE

Team Roles

RESEARCH AND PERSONNEL ▪ Designers undertake a rigorous amount of research to help them learn about the people, problem, and place involved in the project. The place can relate to an environment, such as a design needed for a digital display in a shopping mall versus one intended for the sales floor of a car dealership. Each of those places would have a unique set of challenges, needs, experiences, and outcomes. Place can also relate to the digital domain something is intended for, such as online for public viewing on the Internet or housed within a closed intranet. If the design is intended for Internet access, will people view and see the content while on the go, using a mobile device? If so, how can that on-the-go experience be customized to fit an individual's needs, experiences, and preferences?

All of these factors play into operational research: how the digital experience happens within the intended context, sometimes called in situ, or in the situation. During those kinds of considerations, or in many cases before them, those involved in the project should ask a series of content-related questions to understand what has to get done, the personnel needed to do said tasks, and the time it would take. Designers will walk through these questions to collect answers, either on their own as independent freelancers, or oftentimes with the aid of their fellow creative personnel, administrators, and managers. Maintaining an open line of communication among all involved parties is critical to a project's success. Relying on direct input and feedback from the client goes a long way too.

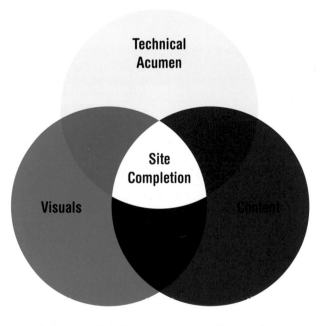

The designer contributes their visual expertise along with a team of content and technology specialists, all of whom work together to complete and launch a website that will meet business, cultural, and strategic needs.

Content-related questions for personnel include:

Who writes the copy?

Where will imagery come from?

Is there a need for motion graphics or video?

What about games?

Would entertainment pull users in, and keep them at the site?

Should users have social networking access or integration?

Are online forms necessary?

Are commercial transactions needed?

Will a Content Management System (CMS) be necessary?

Who handles the long-term maintenance?

Who's responsible whether or not a CMS gets used?

What about existing visual standards, such as brand guidelines?

Project Personnel*

The **art director** sets the conceptual direction for the designers and ensures their work is congruent with that of the photographers, illustrators, developers, programmers, and anyone else involved in the development of a project.

A **designer** visually executes digital material, corporate identity, film titling, and web and multimedia interfaces. (Entry-level designers are one to two years out of school, and will require more hands-on mentoring than a designer or senior designer.)

The **senior designer** is responsible for conceptualization and design of solutions from concept to completion. Sometimes a senior designer oversees and directs junior designers.

A **web designer** establishes and produces a site's look and feel, including site navigation, site design, and visual execution.

A **content strategist** establishes what content needs to be included, its tone of voice, and delivery to the user.

A **copywriter** writes, edits, and proofreads promotional, publicity, and online copy. Experienced copywriters can sometimes be responsible for strategic and conceptual development.

A **content developer** is also known as a web writer or editor, and is responsible for the creation and repurposing of text/graphics/audio content on sites. With written material, they write and/or edit it to work well within a specified space for a given purpose and user.

Photographers create custom photographic images using digital or traditional means, and will oftentimes act as electronic artists by touching up or customizing the images.

Illustrators use any number of rendering tools such as painting and drawing with traditional media, Photoshop and Illustrator with digital media, or a combination of the two as mixed media to create visual narratives, characters, still lifes, information graphics, and any number of other renderings.

Videographers or **video directors** capture motion graphics through digital video and will work with a team of sound engineers, talent and location scouts, editors, writers, and producers to create the final product.

Video editors take the raw video and audio footage, and assemble it into a complete product using tools such as iMovie, Final Cut Pro, Vegas Pro, Sound Forge, or Avid Studio.

The **production manager**, **producer**, or **project manager** is responsible for managing the process (bids, scheduling, production, and delivery) of site production, from concept through completion, including photography, design, digital production, and programming. In some cases, proficiency in digital software such as InDesign, QuarkXPress, Illustrator, and Photoshop as well as programming/development methods such as HTML, CSS, JavaScript, ActionScript, PHP, ASP, and CMS helps them understand a design project, and step in to work on facets as needed.

The **marketing manager** will seek out business opportunities or integrate strategic initiatives into a project.

A **web developer** uses HTML, CSS, JavaScript, ActionScript, and other tools to develop static, dynamic, or interactive websites.

The **web programmer** works solely on the backend, using HTML, CSS, JavaScript, ActionScript, and database tools.

*Adapted from the AIGA, www.designsalaries.org/definitions.shtml

MANAGING THE DESIGN · TEAM ROLES

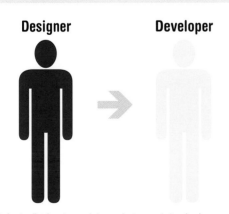

Designer   Developer

Understanding how to complete a project comes in handy when designers deliver some or all of the final build to a third party, whether a printer or developer.

Designer/Developer

However, there are those who design and build the final product.

The Production Cycle Simplified

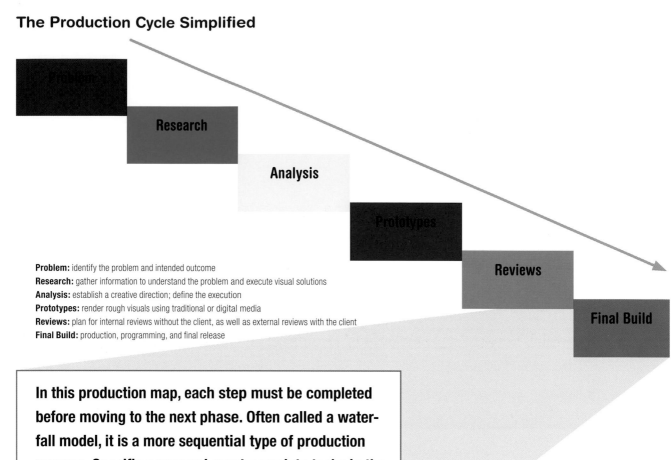

Problem: identify the problem and intended outcome
Research: gather information to understand the problem and execute visual solutions
Analysis: establish a creative direction; define the execution
Prototypes: render rough visuals using traditional or digital media
Reviews: plan for internal reviews without the client, as well as external reviews with the client
Final Build: production, programming, and final release

In this production map, each step must be completed before moving to the next phase. Often called a waterfall model, it is a more sequential type of production process. Specific personnel must complete tasks in the above phases, which get closed off from other personnel. A Gantt chart provides a similar scheme for project visualization and management.

The Design Process

SCOPE AND APPROACH ▪ At the outset, thinking broadly about the project will involve all of the creative parties, rather than focusing solely on navigation and menu interaction, a granular part of the design problem where only designers may find interest. It also helps shape the scope of work, something that must be visible from the outset, whether the design will be for a new site, a revision, an integrated campaign, a small micro-site, or online advertising. This collective brainstorming is especially helpful, since it brings together all team members so that they can review the project, consider the problem, define the scope of work, and plan the attack.

A More Agile Process

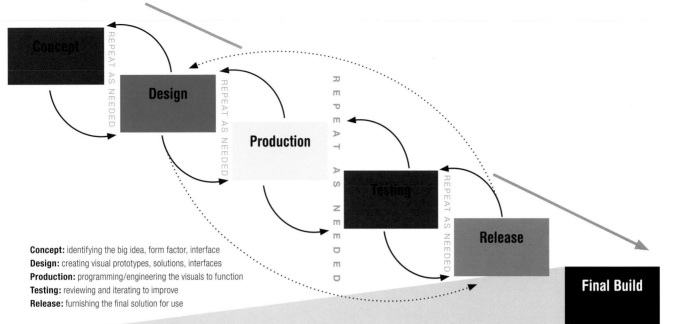

Concept: identifying the big idea, form factor, interface
Design: creating visual prototypes, solutions, interfaces
Production: programming/engineering the visuals to function
Testing: reviewing and iterating to improve
Release: furnishing the final solution for use

Now collaboration happens consistently, and steps overlap with one another to reach the intended goal. Software developers have used this so-called agile method since it is more cyclical in nature: Some facet always gets worked on. Trusting all of the personnel, who will share and exchange work, is tantamount to success in this working method.

Conceptual issues related to the visual communication may come about at this time, and should be heard. However, going too far down the conceptualization and ideation during the scope of work planning can derail the initial planning. But how do you begin working on the design? If all of the content, personnel, and deliverables have been defined from the outset, follow the waterfall approach: a structured and mostly linear process that requires each phase to be completed before moving to the next. Many design agencies follow a waterfall approach, since research and analysis have to happen before defining visual solutions. However, there are cases when text content may not exist, but a deadline looms nearby. How do you move forward without text and imagery?

Consider the approach used by agile software developers: Interactions above processes, Collaboration above negotiation, Feedback, Simplicity.* Agile software developers put an emphasis on function, and preliminary research may not happen as much at the start as it does during the build itself. And the research that does happen may not be as deep and involved as what designers are used to when they are following the waterfall method. Although research is lighter, creating graphics and visual prototypes will still happen, although much quicker in order to get early feedback that fuels the creation of the big idea.

*For further reading: http://agilemanifesto.org and http://alistapart.com/articles/gettingrealaboutagiledesign/

Tim Biskup's redesigned website, by Social Design House, uses larger imagery to put an emphasis on the artist's work. Unlike Biskup's prior website that had much smaller imagery with a center-text layout, the new design gives an updated look and feel with his artwork having a larger presence.

DESIGN AND REDESIGN ▪ Designers will take on one of two types of projects: a new design or a redesign. Each problem will have its own set of objectives, but in many cases, the redesign will offer the creative team a wealth of existing material for assessment. However, a new design will require more preliminary research and discovery to arrive at written content, information architecture, and graphic solutions. In both cases, performing a SWOT analysis will help evaluate the Strengths, Weaknesses, Opportunities, and Threats. By listing items related to each category, a designer can begin to shape creative directions and opportunities using some or all of the results. It is also crucial to identify who will be account-able for the plan, project, actions, and goals necessary to reach the intended purpose. Marion Dosher, Dr. Otis Benepe, Albert Humphrey, Robert Stewart, and Birger Lie developed this method of strategic planning from 1960 to 1970 at the Stanford Research Institute. A number of Fortune 500 companies funded the research to understand why existing planning did not work as intended.

When Landers Miller Design redid the Kidfresh site, they eliminated the all-white background (left) and used a more vibrant green (bottom), indicative of their product packaging.

Questions to ask during a design or redesign:

What is the intended voice?

What is the received voice? Users may understand things differently than the client's intended voice.

What is the existing communication strategy?

Who is the intended audience?

What is being sold or delivered?

How and where will people interact with the brand, product, or service?

Who is the competition?

How are they different?

What do the existing visuals look and feel like?

What types of visual assets exist? Photographic, illustrative, or diagrammatic? How do they contribute to the voice?

Do typographic standards exist, or must they be invented?

Does the written or visual content exist elsewhere? In print? Social media?

Why will people come to the website?

What will get people back again and again?

Questions to ask during a redesign:

Is the navigation easy to follow?

Is the message clearly communicated?

How do the graphics benefit the site both for content and for navigation?

Were you able to navigate through the site without getting lost?

How did the site engage the user, and was this action appropriate to the message?

What was the most interesting aspect of this site?

What brand elements must remain in place?

What brand elements, or other entities, can get replaced?

Structure and Sequence

INFORMATION ARCHITECTURE ■ Designers must create an information system in order to see how wide and deep a site will be. Establishing a hierarchy of information will help facilitate this. Designers will often use a system to delineate primary, secondary, and tertiary information. This can be as simple as a text-based outline where Roman numerals signify the primary content areas, uppercase letters A–Z signify the secondary content areas, and Arabic numerals, bullets, or other symbols mark tertiary content. Something more visual and fluid such as index cards or sticky notes give the designer and even the client the tactile experience of moving and ordering the content. In each case, documentation at every phase will create a history of what had been on the document along with the most recent edits and additions that went into the new document. Saving copies of text outlines, rather than saving over them, creates this working history. And taking photographs of index cards or sticky notes mapped on a wall or other flat surface serves as a helpful documentation method as well.

No single, all-purpose method exists for organizing and labeling the content, so long as a method is used. Information architecture aids not only the design team, but also the end-user, who must navigate the website. If established at the outset at even a minimal level, information architecture will save the designers time and the client money, since the content, navigation, and flow get determined prior to the visual design. And it will ensure that users find what they need when they visit the site, which, in turn, makes everyone happy.

With the information architecture in hand, creating static prototypes will help give structure to how the information lays out visually. Other names for these rough layouts include box models, wireframes, statics, or prototypes. In many cases, these rough designs do not have interactive features, meaning buttons will not work and images will not animate, but the visual skeleton begins to appear in order to put everything in its right place. Models can be built based on top navigation, side navigation, or other real-world matches that users are comfortable with. But in some cases, more experimental approaches can be taken.

Outlining Content

An outline would be quick and easy for structuring a shallow site such as this, with very little primary content. Notes identify what content needs to be reused, omitted, or edited.

I: About us / home – get text from existing home
A. Guiding Principles
B. Our Mission
C. History
D. Board Members – use name and title, no bio text

II: Our Program
A. Recruitment – academic effectiveness, citizenship, leadership potential
B. Partner Schools – get text from existing partners, list CIS schools, but remove CMS
C. Camps – where we send them, list four camps
D. Testimonials

III: In the News
A. Newsletters – no photo here – BICF newsletters
B. Press Releases – no photo here – regional news
1. Charlotte Observer article
2. Charlotte Neighbors article
3. SouthPark magazine article
4. My School Rocks article

IV: Volunteer – no photo – has downloadable forms

V: Contact – no photo – will have Google map link

VI: Right Sidebar – on all pages
A. You Can Help Today – top right for prominence
1. Donate Online – link to FFTC
2. Check / Cash Donation
B. Media – links to Flickr, YouTube
1. Photos
2. Photo slideshow
3. Videos

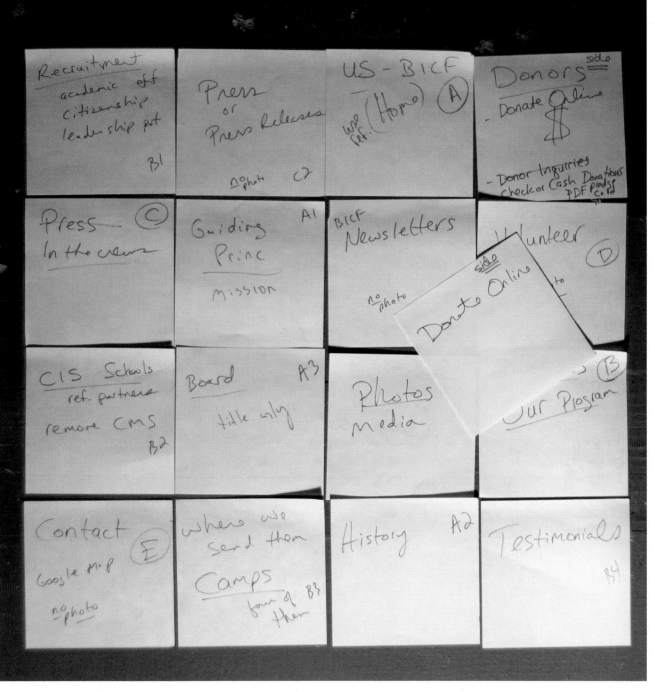

These sticky notes were crafted at the client's office so that the designer and client could walk through the information architecture together. Involving the client in this manner isn't always possible, but it can be advantageous if they possess the highest level of knowledge about the material.

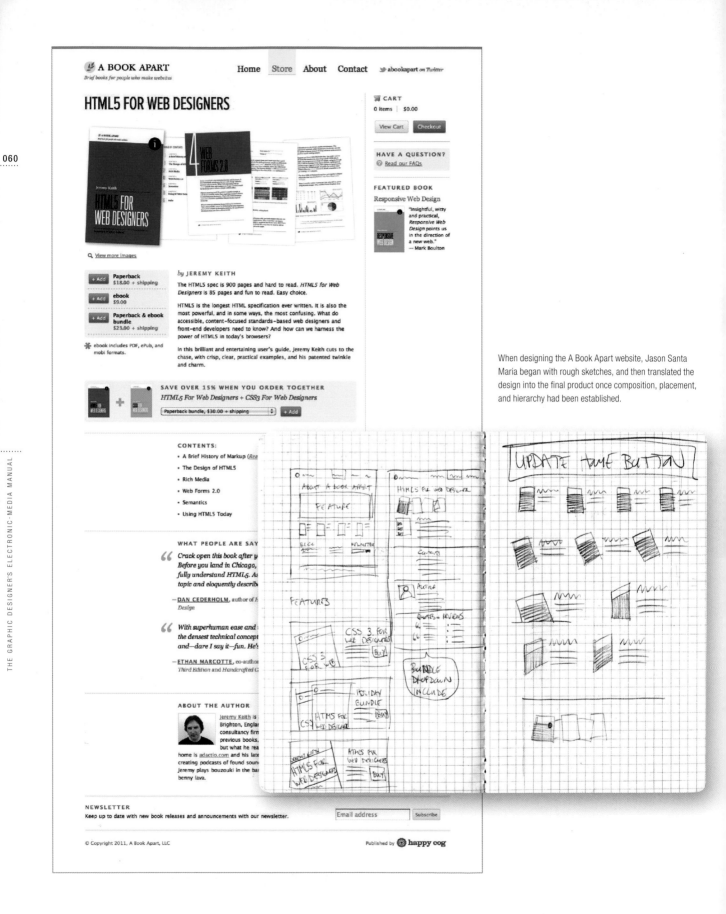

When designing the A Book Apart website, Jason Santa Maria began with rough sketches, and then translated the design into the final product once composition, placement, and hierarchy had been established.

Instrument planned the Nike iDNation website using box models they edited with pencil, all before moving it to a fleshed-out, colored, and final design.

Wireframe Methods

Wireframes can often be called the second sketch, because they follow the initial rough drawings used to visualize the layout. Any of these methods can be used, or combined, in order to achieve the desired result of composing the design.

Rough Media

Drawings: these are quick to make and edit, but are not a formal method for clients

Sticky Notes: speedy, allowing for group interaction and clients participation

Digital Media

Adobe Illustrator, InDesign, Photoshop, or Fireworks: multiple schemes can be built once an initial template gets built, and the boxes can later get colored and styled during the creative stage; buttons can also be created with active links to show users the navigation flow

Microsoft Excel: spreadsheets have cells, making cell divisions quick and easy, and since spreadsheets lack design niceties found in other software, designers can focus on the prototype rather than the look and feel

CSS Box Model: this works very well for developers, and also brings the design one step closer to interaction and linking that comes at the programming stage.

THE GRAPHIC DESIGNER'S ELECTRONIC-MEDIA MANUAL

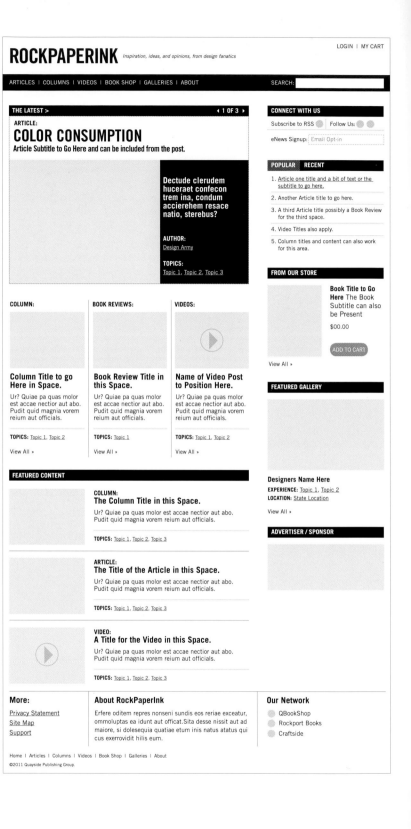

Landers Miller Design built comprehensive box models for the RockPaperInk weblog by rendering them in Adobe Illustrator to look at all of the surface content, including typographic hierarchy.

ROCKPAPERINK

Inspiration, ideas, and opinions, from design fanatics

ARTICLES | COLUMNS | VIDEOS | BOOK SHOP | GALLERIES | ABOUT

SEARCH:

ARTICLE: PATTERN & PALETTE

Date 00, 2011

COLOR CONSUMPTION

Article Subtitle to Go Here and can be included from the post.

Author A. Author, Co-Author Name, Third Author

TOPICS:
Topic 1

◉ Facebook Recommend
◉ Share on Twitter
◉ Email to Friend
◉ +Share This

Caption Copy or Image Credit

Large intro copy to start each article or post. Itatest, sinuscietur aut expland unditibusae. Agnis assi sitas aspelecepero quae occum qui sin culla vid quatqui te exerumr?

Ur? Quiae pa quas molor est accae nectior aut abo. Lest exerum consecu saessit volore la cusdam vendaectem delis qui aceatiur, autem. Ut endae. Ratemoluptat laut in peraecto is aut.

Dollacc uptionseque ommo everum fugia si a susam et ommolorporum fuga. Ut ducideris niaspic ilitati buscipsa quia dem alis quis qui nonsequiae maionem faccum venia dolorest, omnimag namus, etur, a nimil inctur apis veliquis dolo officae.

Ut ducideris niaspic ilitati buscipsa quia dem alis quis qui nonsequiae maionem faccum venia dolorest.

Caption Copy or Image Credit

Caption Copy or Image Credit

Dentis vit eatum doloribus estiur? Qui si ditas anduntiosti berum quod quiam, sedit eosamus andaectis eria nossecte nuscimi nciiscipsum invelique peliquo et eum qui consequia conempore omnit eaquibus quam voluptatur, sed mo blaborecte inctem ari alique sunt volorat.

SOURCE: Secepro ium et adit, natur, oditis voluptus. Ihiliciis vendem aut ut harum exces natqui delit et aligende is nonetur, as doluptatem qui tecae.

LEAVE A COMMENT

Statement about posting procedure and rules. (*) Required Fields.

Your Name*:
Your email*:
Your URL:
Your Comment:

SUBMIT

COMMENTS (X)

Date 00, 2011
Author A. Author

Dollacc uptionseque ommo everum fugia si a susam et ommolorporum fuga. Ut ducideris niaspic ilitati buscipsa quia dem alis quis qui nonsequiae maionem faccum venia dolorest, omnimag namus, etur, a nimil inctur apis veliquis dolo officae.

Date 00, 2011
Author A. Author

Buscipsa quia dem alis quis qui nonsequiae maionem faccum venia dolorest, omnimag namus, etur, a nimil inctur apis veliquis dolo officae.

OTHER ARTICLES OF INTEREST

Article Title to go Here in Space
TOPICS: Topic 1, Topic 2

Article Title to go Here in Space
TOPICS: Topic 1, Topic 2

Article Title to go Here in Space
TOPICS: Topic 1, Topic 2

BROWSE TOPICS

Type Tank

Making & Breaking the Grid

Pattern & Palette

Packaging Essentials

Branding & Identity Essentials

Designer Profiles

Studio Secrets

Fashion Essentials

Handmade

Design Essentials

BROWSE AUTHORS

AUTHOR LISTING LAST NAME ▾

CONNECT WITH US

Subscribe to RSS ◉ | Follow Us: ◉ ◉

eNews Signup: Email Opt-in

FROM OUR STORE

Typography Book Title to Go Here
The Book Subtitle can also be Present

$00.00

ADD TO CART

View All »

ADVERTISER / SPONSOR

With the approved wireframe models in place, Landers Miller moved the design into a more fleshed-out stage, equipped with color, typographic styling, and imagery.

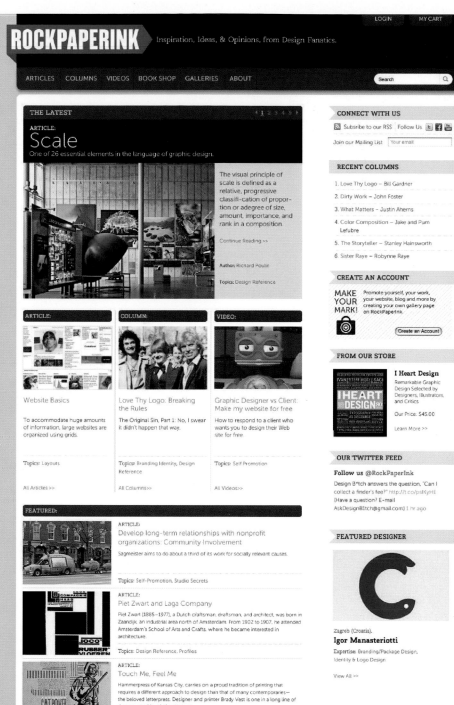

ROCKPAPERINK

Inspiration, Ideas, & Opinions, from Design Fanatics.

LOGIN   MY CART

ARTICLES   COLUMNS   VIDEOS   BOOK SHOP   GALLERIES   ABOUT

Search

THE LATEST   ◄ 1 2 3 4 5 ►

ARTICLE:
Scale
One of 26 essential elements in the language of graphic design.

The visual principle of scale is defined as a relative, progressive classification of proportion or a degree of size, amount, importance, and rank in a composition.

Continue Reading >>

Author: Richard Poulin

Topics: Design Reference

ARTICLE:

Website Basics

To accommodate huge amounts of information, large websites are organized using grids.

Topics: Layouts

All Articles >>

COLUMN:

Love Thy Logo: Breaking the Rules

The Original Sin, Part 1: No, I swear it didn't happen that way.

Topics: Branding Identity, Design Reference

All Columns>>

VIDEO:

Graphic Designer vs Client: Make my website for free

How to respond to a client who wants you to design their Web site for free.

Topics: Self Promotion

All Videos>>

FEATURED:

ARTICLE:
Develop long-term relationships with nonprofit organizations: Community Involvement

Sagmeister aims to do about a third of its work for socially relevant causes.

Topics: Self-Promotion, Studio Secrets

ARTICLE:
Piet Zwart and Laga Company

Piet Zwart (1885–1977), a Dutch craftsman, draftsman, and architect, was born in Zaandijk, an industrial area north of Amsterdam. From 1902 to 1907, he attended Amsterdam's School of Arts and Crafts, where he became interested in architecture.

Topics: Design Reference, Profiles

ARTICLE:
Touch Me, Feel Me

Hammerpress of Kansas City, carries on a proud tradition of printing that requires a different approach to design than that of many contemporaries— the beloved letterpress. Designer and printer Brady Vest is one in a long line of devotees to this printing process.

Topics: Profiles, Handmade

CONNECT WITH US

Subsribe to our RSS   Follow Us

Join our Mailing List   Your email

RECENT COLUMNS

1. Love Thy Logo – Bill Gardner
2. Dirty Work – John Foster
3. What Matters – Justin Ahrens
4. Color Composition – Jake and Pum Lefubre
5. The Storyteller – Stanley Hainsworth
6. Sister Raye – Robynne Raye

CREATE AN ACCOUNT

MAKE YOUR MARK!

Promote yourself, your work, your website, blog and more by creating your own gallery page on RockPaperInk.

Create an Account!

FROM OUR STORE

I Heart Design
Remarkable Graphic Design Selected by Designers, Illustrators, and Critics

Our Price: $45.00

Learn More >>

OUR TWITTER FEED

Follow us @RockPaperInk

Design B*tch answers the question, "Can I collect a finder's fee?" http://t.co/psIKyHE (Have a question? E-mail AskDesignB1tch@gmail.com) 1 hr ago

FEATURED DESIGNER

Zagreb (Croatia).
Igor Manasteriotti

Expertise: Branding/Package Design, Identity & Logo Design

View All >>

MORE INFO:

Contact Us
Privacy Statement
Terms & Copyright
Terms of Use

©2011 Rockport Publishers

ABOUT ROCKPAPER INK:

Inspiration, Ideas, & Opinions, from Design Fanatics

From graphic art to fashion, architecture, and beyond, every topic is fair game, and each contribution builds on the sense of community headed by our experts from around the world.

Learn More >>

OUR NETWORK:

Rockpub.com
Shop our great collection of design books online

Follow Us on Twitter
Keep up with the latest news from RockPaperInk

Join us on Facebook
Consequat, risus eget interdum plac erat, massa

RockPaperInk YouTube Channel
Check out great videos from our contributors.

Concept and Testing

CREATIVE DIRECTION ■ Each of the steps thus far has been about planning, preparation, and organization. Establishing a creative direction is one of the steps to help define what the site will look like, and the creative brief acts as a road map for the client to approve and the design team to follow. Visual or form language should be included within the creative brief to keep everyone on the same page, and establish an end goal for the creative team. Clients who don't know what they want until they see it often get designers to deliver multiple and random visuals over and over again until something works.

But a creative brief helps define what needs to happen, why, and how. The scope of work, SWOT analysis, and information architecture can all factor into the creative brief, but they do not make the creative brief. A well-written and strategic plan happens by way of understanding the involved parties, analyzing their relationships, and considering short- and long-term needs. Online, content comes and goes, and media changes rapidly, so factoring those elements into the creative brief will add even a small degree of longevity. How long should a site last? That depends on the content, users, client, and other external factors. As the name implies, creative briefs may be brief, as in short and to the point. They may also be lengthy, but above all, they should instill a sense of purpose, reason, and potential.

Creative Direction Factors

Personnel Goals

Personnel Duties

Benchmarks

Communication Plan

Scope of Work

Mind Map

Strategy and Objective

Positioning

Nondisclosure Statement

Method of Documentation

Method of Communication via Personnel and Client

Presentation Timeline

Presentation Methods

Creative Direction and the Design Brief*

Include **background information** on you or your firm to highlight your expertise and fit for the job

The **client's situation**, **competition**, and **challenges**

The **client's objectives** and **expectations**

Relating those objectives to the **client's positioning**

An understanding of the **audience**, from current, past, and future perspectives

Any **accessibility** and **usability** issues that the design must address to meet the needs of those with disabilities

The **visual tone** suitable to meet the above needs, whether part of the client's brand standards, supplied text/visual content, or to-be-invented text/visual content

An explanation of **why the specified visual tone should work**, and any issues that require it to change in the future

The **scope of work** with immediate and long-term needs

A **recommended course of action**, which may be broken down into steps built into a calendar

The **creative process you will follow**, and the manner that creative solutions will be delivered, be they rough, refined, or finished; a case study can be shown to illustrate the manner you will go about solving the problem

How many creative solutions will get shown during the preliminary, secondary, and tertiary steps of the development, and how many revisions are allotted

How those creative materials get **presented**, **reviewed**, **documented**, **commented on**, approved, or disapproved

A metric for **gauging the success of the chosen course** (or courses) of action over the short and long terms

Short- and long-term support, specifying how long the agency would service or maintain the site with enhancements, visual changes, or content edits clearly spelled out

The **time**, **money**, and **resources** needed to achieve the goals

*Adapted from "The AIGA Design Business and Ethics" series, 2009.

Mood boards aid the design team with defining a look and feel for the project. At this loose brainstorming phase, any variety of content gets added to a canvas for seeing relationships, tone of image, and personality.

REVIEWING AND PROMOTING ■ Evaluation should happen throughout the planning, ideation, and design process. Those on the creative team should constantly check in with one another to keep an open line of communication, making sure that milestones have been completed and unmet needs have been accounted for. Art directors and creative directors should go through rigorous quality assurance to ensure the conceptual and visual direction they've established has been implemented. Clients will factor into these reviews as well, and at some point outside subjects may enter the picture through usability studies. Usability studies (or heuristic evaluations) consider functionality from top to bottom by putting working prototypes in front of an audience and giving them a task to complete. They are similar to focus groups, where facilitators ask people questions to establish a qualitative and quantitative understanding of the materials at hand. And as with any design project, it's important to understand the audience that will interact with the design, and make sure the test subjects match up very closely to the designated profile or profiles. While some creative firms take it upon themselves to perform these studies, doing so internally with people who worked on the project, getting outside opinions can certainly offer fresh insight. In the beginning, test subjects share their expectations through a prestudy interview. Questions can address qualitative issues: the user's knowledge of the site, material, product, and so on; what she expects to see when she interacts with the design; what she'd find rewarding when

she interacts with the design; what she'd want to avoid. Or quantitative issues can be shared too: how long the user expects the process to take; the number of steps, links, or menus she would have to go through; what she might deem as too long or too many of the aforementioned. It's important that test subjects understand that they are not under examination; it's not a test for them to pass or fail. If anything, the creative and design team stands to succeed or fail. Facilitators lay out a series of tasks for subjects to complete. The tasks may be listed in a numerical order where items get completed one at a time before moving to the next. Scenarios may also be given: It's your mother's birthday, go to this site and find her a present. With shopping, you may have to purchase, exchange, and return something online. For communications, opening, reading, replying, and forwarding email may happen. Facilitators document the test subjects' actual experience with the site. Screen recorders can capture the users' cursor movement, keyboard strokes, and link clicking. Video recorders may capture the users' facial expressions, body language, and spoken words. In the end, the facilitator conducts a postmortem interview: Did you enjoy the experience, was there anything missing, did things work well or poorly, what about the graphics, what would you improve, how would you see this site changing in the future, or would you use this site again in the future. Physical issues such as where the study takes place, how the user will be situated during the test, and the technology to be used play into preparing and conducting usability tests.

Heuristic or usability labs such as this, allow researchers to analyze how digital designs, such as software and websites, perform. Recording equipment will monitor the user's facial and body movement, while screen recording captures their mouse movement and clicking.

Evaluation Considerations

The first thing that happens when we see an interface is just that: We see it. A number of questions come into play for the user, who will then choose to interact with the media or not. Clicking, dragging, pushing, and pulling content happens during the experience. Words may get typed, deleted, or swiped. And in the end, the user may have made a purchase, read or sent an email, looked at or commented on photographic imagery, shared a video, or backed up her computer. The possibilities are now unlimited, with users finding entertainment, education, research, games, or jobs online. Each possibility has its own set of rich experiences.

Appearance

Attractiveness. Does the interface look appealing enough to engage the user, keep her there, and keep her coming back?

Composition. Does the design look well thought out? Are things consistent?

Appropriateness. Does the interface meet the user's expectations?

Surprise. If the design looks different, does this surprise the user in a good way, or repel her because the design doesn't look appropriate?

Play. Does the design promise some sense of excitement that would result from interacting with it?

Motivation. How can the user be spurred to engage with the design whether by reading the content, clicking through links, or dabbling through the material? Special offers can spur shoppers, and rich media such as games, music, or videos can entice those looking for entertainment.

Content

Brand. Is the brand identity visible and credible?

Copy. Is the written material suitable for the content and context? Does the language make sense to the user? Do headlines entice readers?

Imagery. Are images of good quality? Are they positioned within the layout in a well-composed manner?

Multiplicity. Can content be reached from a number of channels?

Search. Is a search field quickly accessible for users to input a query?

Site Index. Can a complete overview of the site be delivered to see the complete lay of the land?

Typography. Is the content readable? Is the typography appropriate?

Interaction

Flow. Does the flow from one content area to another deliver what was promised?

Navigation. Can the user recognize where she is? Get back to where she came from? And see where to go next?

Reassurance. Do cues exist to acknowledge where the user is, where she came from, and what's next? This is especially valuable with commercial, shopping, and financial transactions.

Undo. Is there a way to rewind or revert to a preliminary state?

Saving. Will content that's been entered be saved for later use or retrieval?

Exporting. Can content the user input be saved outside of the existing design for use elsewhere?

Driving users to the digital experience remains one of the most challenging parts of the design process. By building promotion and traffic generation into the early planning and design phases, promotion gets built into the entire design strategy. This ensures a unified approach, and also creates checks and balances among team members: Content creators and editors who capture photos or video will benefit from knowing early on that some videos may need to appear on YouTube. It can be easy to deliver just one component of a design solution, such as a website or email newsletter. But clients benefit most when they receive the total package: planning, strategy, visual content, promotion, and even ongoing maintenance and monitoring. Banks Wilson, president and creative director at Studiobanks, reinforces the need for delivering a total design: "For us, building sites and helping clients reach their target audience go hand in hand. From the beginning of a project, we're looking at the various resources and tools that will help us connect most effectively with that audience. We're always focused on how we're helping our clients meet their goals and objectives, so we're not just trying to build a quality site, app, or digital platform—we're trying to build these components in a way that will inspire engagement and truly draw in visitors." Designers and agencies that recognize these issues will deliver an added value to their clients, as well as the users who interact with the media. But the methods for creating and delivering these promotional vehicles will continue to change, as Eric Karjaluoto, creative director at smashLAB, suggests: "A greater variety of screen sizes, faster processors, and browser capabilities, will all affect how we build sites, alongside the conventions we employ. Make no mistake, though; new conventions will emerge so that we can all feel comfortable using this technology."

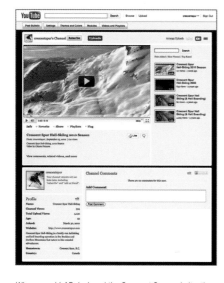

When smashLAB designed the Crescent Spur website, they also delivered three alternate avenues for users to experience the brand: Facebook page, YouTube channel, and email newsletter. All of these touchpoints are digital, but maintain a relationship between the brand and consumer.

Written articles and blog posts have become the norm for small and large organizations, as well as individuals. Jason Santa Maria has created a repository of information at his online portfolio, with articles dedicated to the hows and whys behind visual media and culture. Words and phrases in articles such as these can help one to gain traction through search engines and social media such as Google+, Twitter, and Facebook.

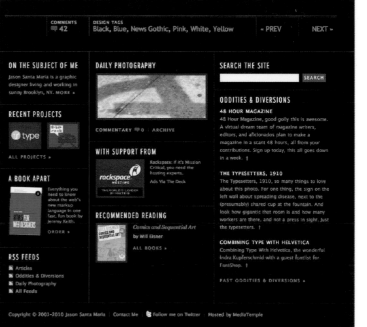

Chapter

3 FOR

MAT + LAYOUT

"Sketchbooks are not about being a good artist;
they're about being a good thinker."

—JASON SANTA MARIA

The Format

FORMAT DERIVATIONS ▪ A designer brings visual elements together in the format, and if there's one thing that all digital media has in common, it's variety. The wide variety of screen dimensions and definitions affect how a design gets displayed for the viewer. A 15-inch (38.1 cm) screen will provide a smaller viewing area than an 8-inch (20.3 cm) computer screen. And a standard 11-inch (28 cm) computer screen will display content differently than an 11-inch (28 cm) high-definition screen. Handheld devices such as mobile phones and tablets present an altogether different challenge, since those devices will shrink a website to fit the screen; although in some cases, a designer and developer can work together to have one site prepared for desktop computers and another for mobiles and tablets.

Each of these digital devices has a different sized screen, and will render digital media in a different way as a result.

Thanks to hardware and software that lets users enlarge a website, designs can now change size in order to accommodate the viewer's needs. Pinching and expanding two fingers on a tablet enlarges the Cornell Department of Architecture site by Paul Soulellis.

Each of these formats has a different sized screen measured in pixel width and height. They will render media in a different way as a result of the different sizes. If the screen allows rotation from landscape to portrait, then it will alter the layout even further. And if the device has a high resolution display, images and text will appear sharper than on the standard 72-dpi display.

ASPECT RATIOS ■ Digital displays have different types of aspect ratios. An aspect ratio is the relationship between the width to the height, and resembles $x{:}y$, where x is the width and y is the height. The figure is spoken as x to y, x by y, or merely $x\,y$. Screen sizes often get expressed as aspect ratios. A screen or image size of 640×480 pixels has an aspect ratio of 4:3. The 4:3 aspect ratio was commonly used in television until the advent of widescreen displays with their wider aspect ratio of 16:9. Some television manufacturers have 21:9 screen sizes, but 16:9 continues to be manufactured. Still photography has used aspect ratios of 3:2, 4:3, and most recently the widescreen 16:9, to better match the dimensions of personal computers and home theaters. Movies are formatted at 2.39:1, 16:9, or 1.85:1 and 16:9 displays have the best compatibility because of their wider format.

Format Considerations

Will the site appear on a digital display, a projector, or both? Knowing if the site must scale from a small size to a large size can impact key design choices, as well as the final programming and development.

Is there a particular screen size in mind? Find out if the site will get viewed in a restricted capacity. A site meant for digital display in a large auditorium will have different needs than a site meant exclusively for mobile devices.

What about printing the content? Sometimes a person will want a hard copy, in which case he'll print the site out and will expect to see on paper what he sees on the screen. Be sure to meet those needs, or deliver a print-only version of the site.

Common Aspect Ratios

4:3

3:2

16:9

16:10

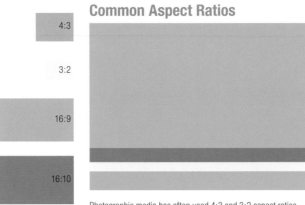

Photographic media has often used 4:3 and 3:2 aspect ratios. The 16:9 and 16:10 aspect ratios are often called widescreen, and the 16:10 aspect ratio has become popular on laptops.

16:10 Digital Display Dimensions

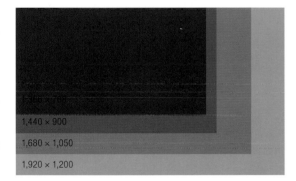

1,280 × 768
1,440 × 900
1,680 × 1,050
1,920 × 1,200

4:3 Digital Display Dimensions

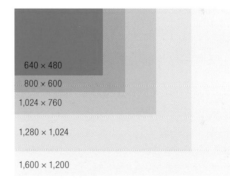

640 × 480
800 × 600
1,024 × 760
1,280 × 1,024
1,600 × 1,200

Cinematic Aspect Ratios

21:9

1.85:1

16:9

16:10

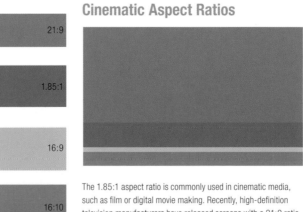

The 1.85:1 aspect ratio is commonly used in cinematic media, such as film or digital movie making. Recently, high-definition television manufacturers have released screens with a 21:9 ratio, yielding an extremely wide landscape presentation.

FORMAT + LAYOUT · THE FORMAT

0+1+1+2+3+5+8+13+21

13 point body text

21 point subhead

34 point headline

In this Fibonacci series, the first set of integers 0 and 1 are added together to arrive at the third integer of 1. Taking 1 and adding it to 1 gives you the fourth integer. To get the next number in the series, add 13 to 21 to get 34. Sizing type with this system can deliver a noticeable hierarchy. Instead of points, pixels would also work as a unit.

In this hierarchical composition, the left and right column widths have been built based on a Fibonacci ratio of 21 (left) and 34 (right).

PROPORTION ▪ Mathematical proportions can help create relationships when composing in digital formats. The rule of thirds breaks it into a three-by-three zone, equipped with nine individual units. Each of those units can be further broken down into its own set of units to create more areas for placing visual elements. Mathematical proportions rely on numerical relationships. The Fibonacci sequence uses an integer sequence where subsequent numbers get added to the preceding one. The golden mean is another method for breaking up space and creating harmony among different compositional zones. No matter the method used, the space should be broken up in a decisive manner using a well-intended system. The organization should make sense given the format, audience, content, purpose, and brand, and doing so ensures that the final compositions match a real-world use.

Another method of developing proportional relationships relies on letting the content dictate the solution. This requires having key elements in hand, such as text-based content used for menus, submenus, feature articles, and footers. Taking that material and using it as your kit of parts will create a direct relationship between the material that goes into the design and the format where it gets displayed.

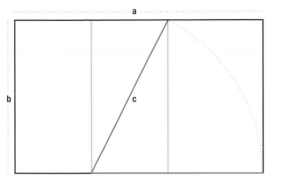

The golden ratio, expressed here as a golden rectangle, has one long component (a) juxtaposed by a shorter one (b). The hypotenuse of a square's half-rectangle (c) is used to construct the golden rectangle by rotating it to the base. Swiss architect Le Corbusier relied on this and other mathematical systems to create a sense of harmony and order in his designs.

Dividing a composition into three equal parts helps to position elements within the format.

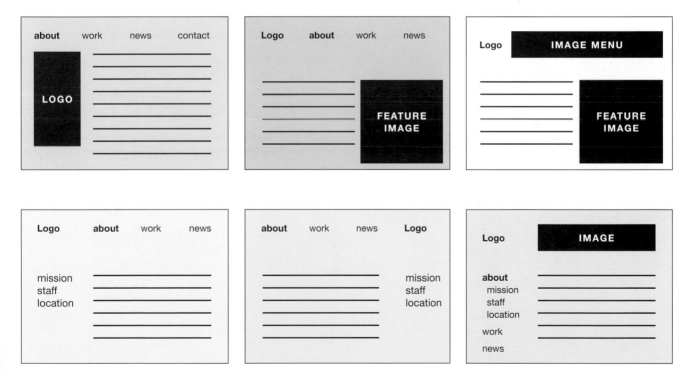

Text can get placed and sized within a number of layouts to examine compositional opportunities.

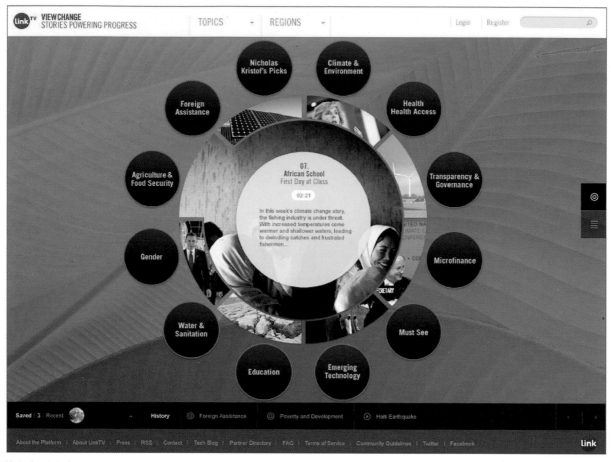

Method's website for the viewchange.org positions a centered menu in front of the viewer so they can easily access all of the content.

Composition Basics

SYMMETRY AND ASYMMETRY ▪ Designers continue to have a split vote on the classic composition principle known as symmetry. For many, it represents an ideal and simplified way of composing elements within space since humans have a natural inclination to operate as vertically erect and mobile beings when they stand and move. Centered compositions are confrontational, delivering visual elements directly toward the viewer by placing them within the vertical or horizontal axis. Symmetrical compositions deliver a confrontational formalism to save users from too much scanning and guessing.

A Doritos website preloader, as featured at Big Spaceship's Pretty Loaded website, composes elements around a radial axis with different sized chips, resulting in a radial composition that lacks radial symmetry.

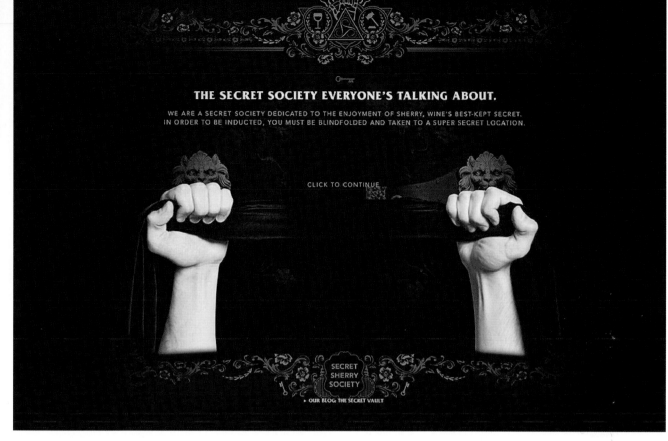

Archrival's website for the Sherry Council of America uses a symmetrical composition at the gateway. This confronts the viewer with all of the information he must enter to view the site, and readies a faux blindfold for all entrants.

The large photograph on the left and smaller typographic element on the right asymmetrically balance Big Spaceship's website for the *New York Times* in College.

Voice used a largely asymmetrical composition when designing the Skala Bakery website.

082

Asymmetrical compositions have no symmetrical parts. Instrument's layout for Invisible Creature positions a large feature image within the format, dominating the composition to create an asymmetrical layout.

In bilateral symmetry, the left side mirrors the right. Although not a literal example of bilateral symmetry, splitting this photograph of a keyboard down the middle will result in the left and right sides possessing nearly the same compositional elements.

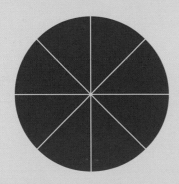

Radial symmetry possesses a trait similar to a birthday cake or pizza, whereby any line drawn across the format creates two reflective parts.

BALANCE ▪ Whether symmetrical or asymmetrical in form, balance is one of the key elements in assembling a composition. Symmetrical compositions will have all of the equilibrium placed within the format's center, with uniform elements on either side, oftentimes appearing as a mirror image. Achieving balance in asymmetrical compositions, however, requires more patience and care. Proportional systems are one of the ways to help achieve balance.

The printer Alfred Tolmer published one of the premier treatises on balance in *Mise En Page: The Theory and Practice of Layout*. In *Mise en Page* (the French term for layout), Tolmer suggested that designers could only achieve compositional balance through feeling. Size, contour, color, value, texture, position, and even the person and his viewing conditions can all affect balance. But even when designers achieve Zenlike moments, and craft balanced compositions, changes in screen dimension and proportion can wreak havoc on the phenomenon. Despite these complications and the fact that no formula exists to achieve compositional balance, that doesn't mean it should be ignored.

The large photograph gets offset by disparate chunks of text content in Silverpoint's website for the American School of Warsaw.

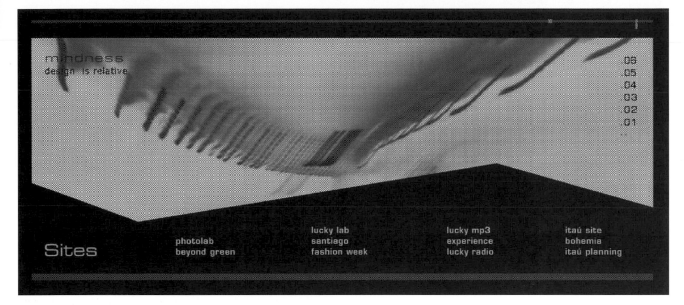

Belmer Negrillo's experimental website Mindness.net possesses asymmetrical balance, since the large texture on the top balances out the geometrically shaped menu on the bottom.

The opening of Archrival's Travis Pastrana Super Mega Nitro Jump game has a symmetrical balance since the left and right sides appear to weigh the same. However, the tilted sign at the top throws things off, delivering a tenuous feeling.

Despite, or because of, the limited amount of visual elements, the Landwest website by Christian Helms seems to have everything in the right place: from the top navigation to the large photograph with text content offset by a tree on the right.

NEGATIVE SPACE ▪ Compositional areas without text, image, or graphic elements are called white space or negative space. Designers should strive to use white space functionally, as too much can make a composition look empty and sterile. Many designers consider even a small amount of white space a tool for making a composition sophisticated, this in contrast to layouts with too much information, which may appear busy or cluttered. Functionally, white space creates contrast between the to-be-seen visual elements and areas of rest or stasis: White space can create halos around or near areas that should get attention. And in terms of developing a conceptual approach, white space can further an underlying message the designer hopes to communicate to the viewer.

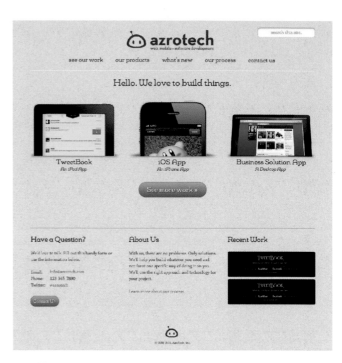

Joshua Mauldin's website for Azrotech doesn't literally use white space, as much as it uses the negative space around the "See more work" button. Offsetting the call to action in this way helps get the user's attention, spurring him to move forward through the website.

Christian Helms' Austin Beerworks website frames a center-formatted photograph amid crisp areas of negative space on the left and right sides, to bring focus to the Community message.

TRICKS

HALF PIPE

EVOLUTION

LIFESTYLE

SILVERTON

+ Shaun secretly dials in a list of new tricks.

⊞ FRONT DOUBLE CORK TEN

⊞ SWITCH BACK 900

⊞ DOUBLE BACK RODEO

⊞ CAB DOUBLE CORK TEN

⊞ DOUBLE MCTWIST

SHAUN PUSHED THE SPORT WITH ANOTHER TRICK

Archrival's website for Shaun White has photographic and text content, framed by negative space that begins at the photograph's bottom and continues toward the right hemisphere's body text.

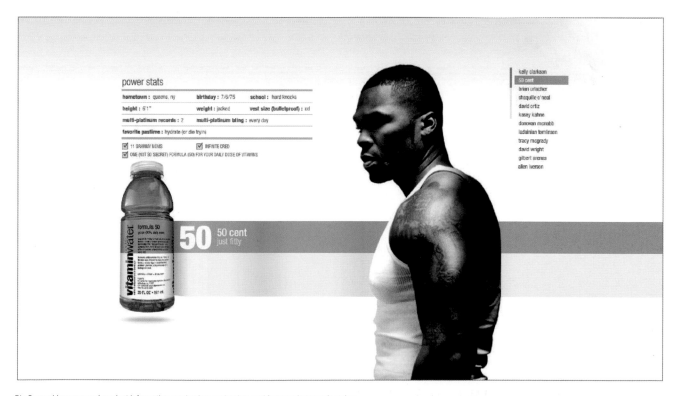

Big Spaceship composed product information, packaging, navigation, and feature photography using ample negative space to give viewers the feeling that Glacéau delivers a pure and healthy product.

LAYOUT CONVENTIONS ▪ People have become accustomed to experiencing websites in a given way, based on accepted standards. Some of these standards have developed over the years based on human-computer interaction assessment, such as work done by Jakob Nielsen. In 1998, the *New York Times** called Nielsen "the guru of web page usability" and he has continued to live up to that title. Nielsen's website Useit.com showcases a number of reports including some that cover web usability, user preferences, and testing social media features. As far back as 1998, Nielsen has championed sites like Amazon.com and Yahoo!, both of which showed people as much information as possible when they arrived at the site. And even today, most people will reference Amazon.com when they talk about experiencing a website because of its top-tier menus, featured products placed at or near the center, and wide variety of tertiary information placed sporadically. Sites like Amazon.com that adhere to a logical and consistent formula, give users a predictable experience that keeps them from getting lost or overwhelmed. Eric Karjaluoto, creative director at smashLAB, champions simplicity when approaching design problems: "Given how complex screen experiences can be, a lot of them frustrate and confuse users. Therefore, [an] enjoyable user experience starts with making a commitment to create logical, clear, and seemingly obvious design solutions."

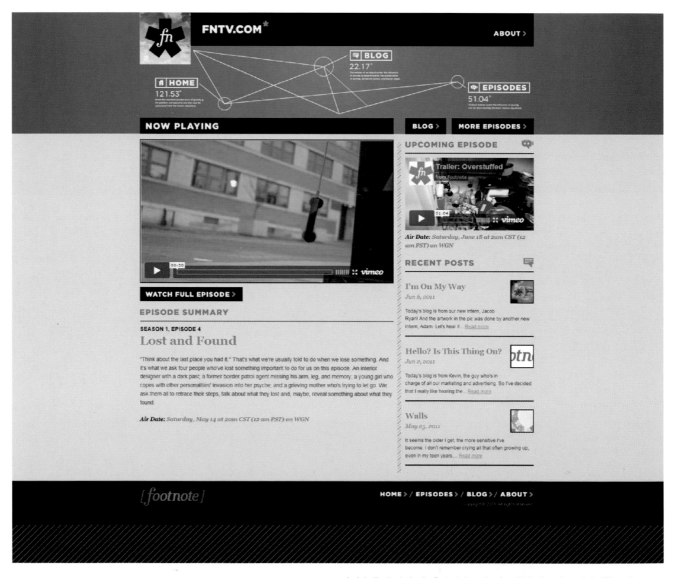

* The *New York Times*, July 13, 1998, "Making Web Sites More 'Usable' Is Former Sun Engineer's Goal"

Archrival's site design for Footnote has a header with the logo, the website URL, and an interactive Flash menu. Hovering over Home, Blog, or Episodes gently moves the menu item and highlights it white to signal it's active.

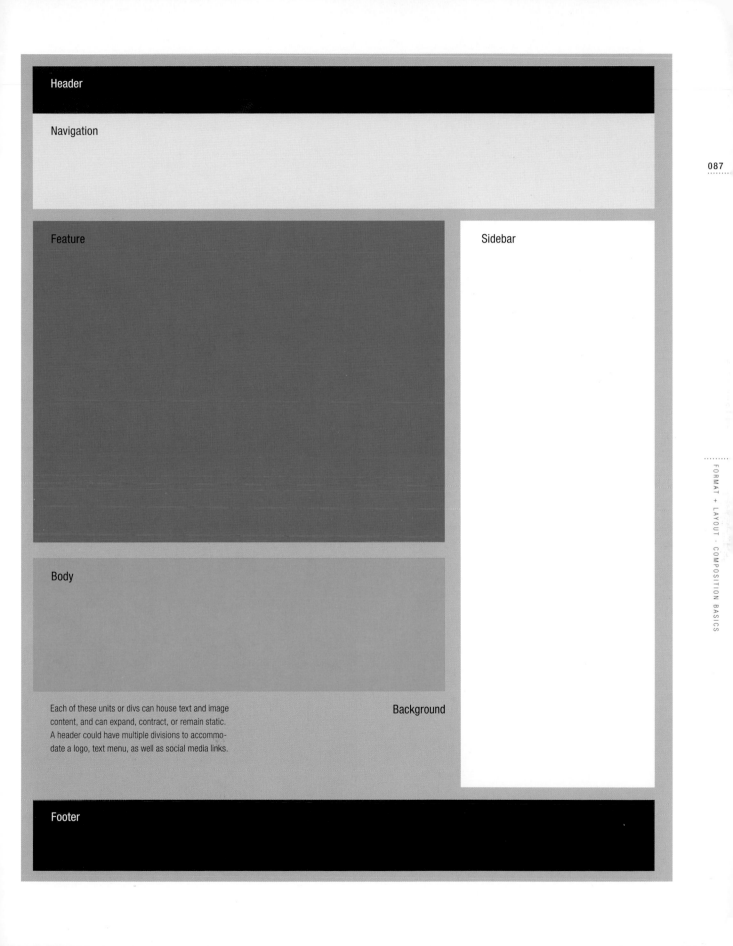

Header

Navigation

Feature

Sidebar

Body

Each of these units or divs can house text and image content, and can expand, contract, or remain static. A header could have multiple divisions to accommodate a logo, text menu, as well as social media links.

Background

Footer

Voice's website for Longview wines pairs a scenic outdoor image with a vertical navigation scheme on the left. The large menu typography helps balance out the composition, and also makes the menu choices clearly visible.

An entertainment venue such as the XL Center in Hartford, Connecticut, uses a top-navigation system, as well as a featured event navigation system where information about the Taylor Swift concert gets accessed by clicking the blue button. By giving users these choices, carbonhouse presents everything but the kitchen sink.

Social Design House uses a top-navigation system that allows their portfolio images to span the width of the format. A left- or right-side menu would interrupt the large images, or worse yet, make them smaller.

Firebelly's website for the Neighborhood Parents Network includes both text and icon-based menu items, to help visitors connect an image to the content they're viewing.

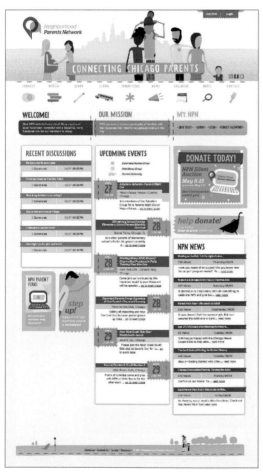

Composition Tools

ELEMENTS AND TAGS ■ On the web, type and image come together within a CSS box model. Rectangular boxes get generated for elements within the source document or source code, and every box has its own content area to house text, imagery, or motion graphics. The box may contain a margin, border, and padding, and be filled with background colors or imagery in addition to the element placed within it. Boxes may be placed within one another as children of the superseding parent box, and each box can have its own set of interactive elements that may relate to elements within the assigned page or another page within the existing site.

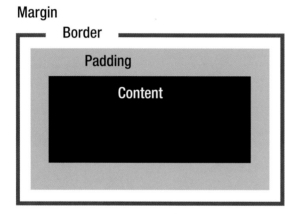

A box can have multiple edges, all of which extend outward from the content box edge.

An image we see in one way on the screen gets placed in a variety of manners within a box. In most cases, you want the image to scale proportionally to the box, and in other cases, you could use it as a pattern.

When Silverpoint designed the Marlborough Summer School website, they used a wide variety of text styles, all tagged in the HTML and defined in the CSS.

In HTML, tags delineate one item from another, such as those used for typographic styling. Two types of tags exist: start and end tags. The contents get placed between the start and end tags, and in the case of typography, can change how a piece of text looks. Each tag has a name that in most cases relates to a semantic property. The <p> tag, for instance, denotes a paragraph, which will sit within the body tag of <body>.

This text has been housed in a paragraph tag.

<p>This text has been housed in a paragraph tag.</p>

The text between the <p> start tag and the </p> end tag creates a paragraph element.

This text has been housed in an emphasis tag.

<em>This text has been housed in an emphasis tag.</em>

The <em> tagged text would appear in italic.

This text has been housed in a strong tag.

<strong>This text has been housed in a strong tag.</strong>

The <strong> tagged text would appear in bold.

THE GRID ▪ Ultimately, these elements with their tags need to be placed within units, intervals, and super units. And the grid acts as a system to assemble all of the parts in a unified manner. In print, the grid remains mostly static, since the page size is fixed and unchangeable. But the wealth of screen sizes in the digital world necessitates adaptable solutions that can change to meet the smallest mobile device, middle-of-the-road tablets or laptops, and perhaps large screens found on desktop computers or televisions. Creating grids that adapt to certain media requires a degree of backend work in the form of media queries that set a layout depending on the source, with the resultant grid layout (or order) known as source order.

When the creative team redesigned the SlideRoom site, they used a more complex twelve-column grid to create relationships between larger feature items and smaller secondary ones. The grid carries over through all parts of the site.

Other grids place elements in an arrangement best for landscape orientations, such as those on desktop and laptop computers or portrait orientations commonly found on tablets. Tripleships' Tanzaku WordPress theme easily adapts to wide or long formats by changing its columnar layout to meet the screen width.

Track or Height

Grid Line

Grid Element

Track or Height

Grid Cell

Grid Line

Track or Height

Grid Line

Track or Width

Track or Width

Grid Line

Grid Line

Grid Line

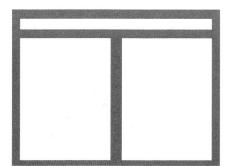

Some grids place elements in a manner suitable for portrait orientations used by tablets and phones. A two-column layout, used by social networks such as Twitter, can adapt to a desktop or tablet browser, positioned in a landscape or portait orientation.

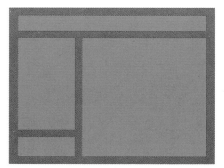

Many web designers rely on hierarchically delineating elements to accommodate content. The grid elements can sit in a fixed position with a static size, or change depending on the user's computer display or window size. Common frameworks can use menus on the top, sides, or in both places to deliver a predictable experience for the user.

In this three-column grid, each unit can house text or image content, and has an interval between each column.

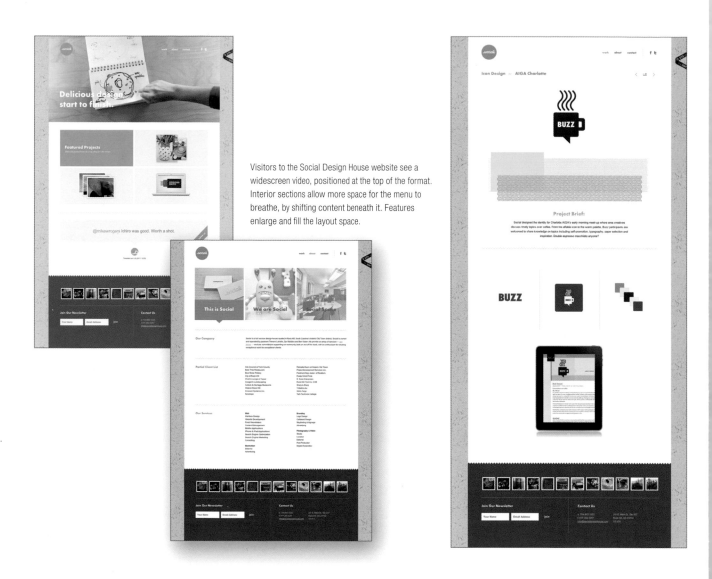

Visitors to the Social Design House website see a widescreen video, positioned at the top of the format. Interior sections allow more space for the menu to breathe, by shifting content beneath it. Features enlarge and fill the layout space.

SEQUENCE AND PACING ▪ For multipart designs, with various elements linked together, designers have to consider how one interface compares or contrasts with another. As visual elements appear, reappear, or disappear, a visual rhythm occurs for the viewer, who will experience these similarities and differences as either a hindrance or a help. Each new link visited could have enough differentiation to foster deeper interest, and keep users at the site. Visitor retention like this can help everyone involved. Layout changes can also signify new content areas, whereby the user experiences a new page the way he would experience a new room with many of the same elements having modified placement. Ultimately, pacing creates differentiation, with an element looking somewhat similar, very similar, or completely different from its predecessor. On the other hand, the user might not notice the changes at all. They could be so subtle and hidden so as not to alarm the user. But take caution, because subtle changes can create too much variety, and in effect, create boredom for the user.

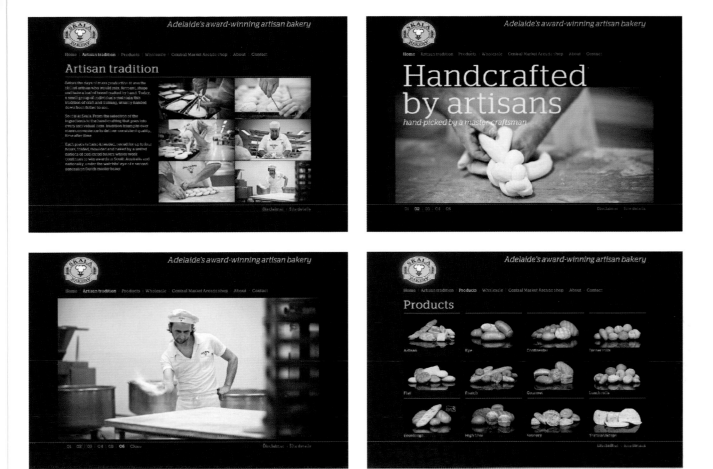

As visitors go deeper into the Skala Bakery website by Voice, image sizes change, feature text gets added, and color photography gets introduced upon visiting their products.

The Nomadic by Design website maintains a three-column layout, but users encounter large photographs overtaking the layout as they move through the site.

When MODE designed the Checkers website, they took adaptability into account because many consumers use their mobile devices to locate nearby stores, restaurants, and shopping outlets.

As an added bonus, mobile users of Checkers' site can get distance and directions to the nearest restaurant.

Other factors begin to weigh into the creation of a site if adaptability is necessary: cost, ergonomics, and tangibility. Will it cost more to have a site adapt across a phone, tablet, and personal computer? Doing so would require multiple designs, or more conveniently, a prebuilt method of changing one design into a format for the other two. Either way, that requires additional time and money. With user personas established, how will they primarily interact with the device?

As of this writing, tablet users account for nearly as much Internet use as mobile phone users. And if that number continues to increase, many sites will have to adapt to their ergonomic needs: no mouse and a virtual keyboard instead of a physical one. Those last two issues tap into tangibility. Devices without external input devices such as mice and keyboards require different user needs, and also use screen space much differently than devices with said external devices.

Page or image scaling also factors into how a site adapts. Many web browsers, especially those on personal computers, allow users to resize windows. And users who connect their laptops to external displays also have the ability to enlarge a site's viewing area. Fluid layouts are one of the ways to accommodate these instances, but proportional scaling is another. By proportionally scaling a site to keep its width-to-height ratio as the screen expands, the design will maintain the same format, no matter the window or display size.

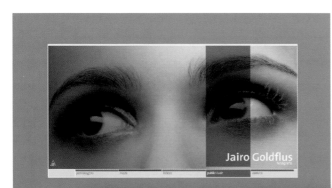

Belmer Negrillo's website for Jairo Goldflus maintains the same width-to-height ratio no matter the window size. A line of code scales the site's width and height to enlarge or shrink, but always maintains the aspect ratio.

Christian Helms' website for Austin Beerworks has an unusually wide format that gets hidden when a window is smaller than its native width. But as the window expands, it reveals more content.

A site or image which scales proportionally, keeps all of the content within that same aspect ratio, no matter the window or display size. Note the square shape of the sticky notes in the original photograph.

If the aspect ratio is *not* locked in the backend, the site or images will squash or squish, thereby distorting content. In the top example, the image has been compressed down, squashing the original aspect ratio. The bottom example shows an image compressed stretched horizontally. These mistakes should be avoided.

Moving from one content area to another used to happen through clicks, drags, scrolls, or a combination input through a device or keyboard. As digital devices continue to evolve with touchscreen interfaces and high-definition displays, new interaction methods and new formats will pervade the visual landscape. A format that has become increasingly acceptable is the long-scrolling layout. In the late 1990s, a website measuring 2,000 pixels or taller was considered far too long for reasons relating to speed and scrolling. Digital download was a fraction of what it is today, and users relied on 28k or 56k dial-up modems. Computers could download text and imagery at an average of 33.3 kilobits per second. But loading a long website that reaches well past the 7,000-pixel length is no problem thanks to the 30 megabits per second (1,000 times the speed of outdated dial-up modems) that users have become accustomed to through digital Internet services such as Time Warner and Verizon.

But even with fast Internet connections, scrolling down infinitely didn't catch on until the 2000s, and reached its zenith in 2007 when designers created long-scrolling portfolio websites. Today, they're still popular, thanks in part to the hands-on experience we have with tablets and smartphones. Their touchscreen interface allows us to swipe with our finger. A fast swipe will move content quickly and, at times, continuously if a momentum feature is enabled. Software such as Adobe Photoshop has this feature built-in, calling it Flick Panning, to make an image glide for long durations with the swipe of the mouse or a flick of the finger. These interactions have become normal for some users, and may one day become the norm. Eric Karjaluoto, creative director at smashLAB, suggests that conventions help users and designers: "On the whole, conventions are a good thing. They generally only demand reconsideration when the situation substantially changes. A good example of this is a large, multiuser touch display. Where do you put your navigation when there's no real top or bottom (i.e., when it's configured as a flat table)? Which way do you orient the type, knowing that people can approach from any direction? How do you deal with multiple people touching the screen at the same time? We still don't really know the answers to these questions, but they open up some interesting debates." Format conventions have become acceptable, especially in the printed realm. But even there, paper is three-dimensional, and can be flipped, folded, molded, and cut into a variety of shapes—all with differing textures and colors. The digital realm may one day deliver similar tactile and physical experiences. But for the time being, most of what we see and experience will be in flatland.

Nitai Whitehurst's photography portfolio, designed by Twofold Creative, has handy buttons that save users the trouble of scrolling the lengthy site by dropping or jumping from one content area to another.

An infinite canvas allows you to scroll left and right to browse articles, and then up and down to read/continue the single article itself. This has become a convention for reading magazines on tablets such as the iPad.

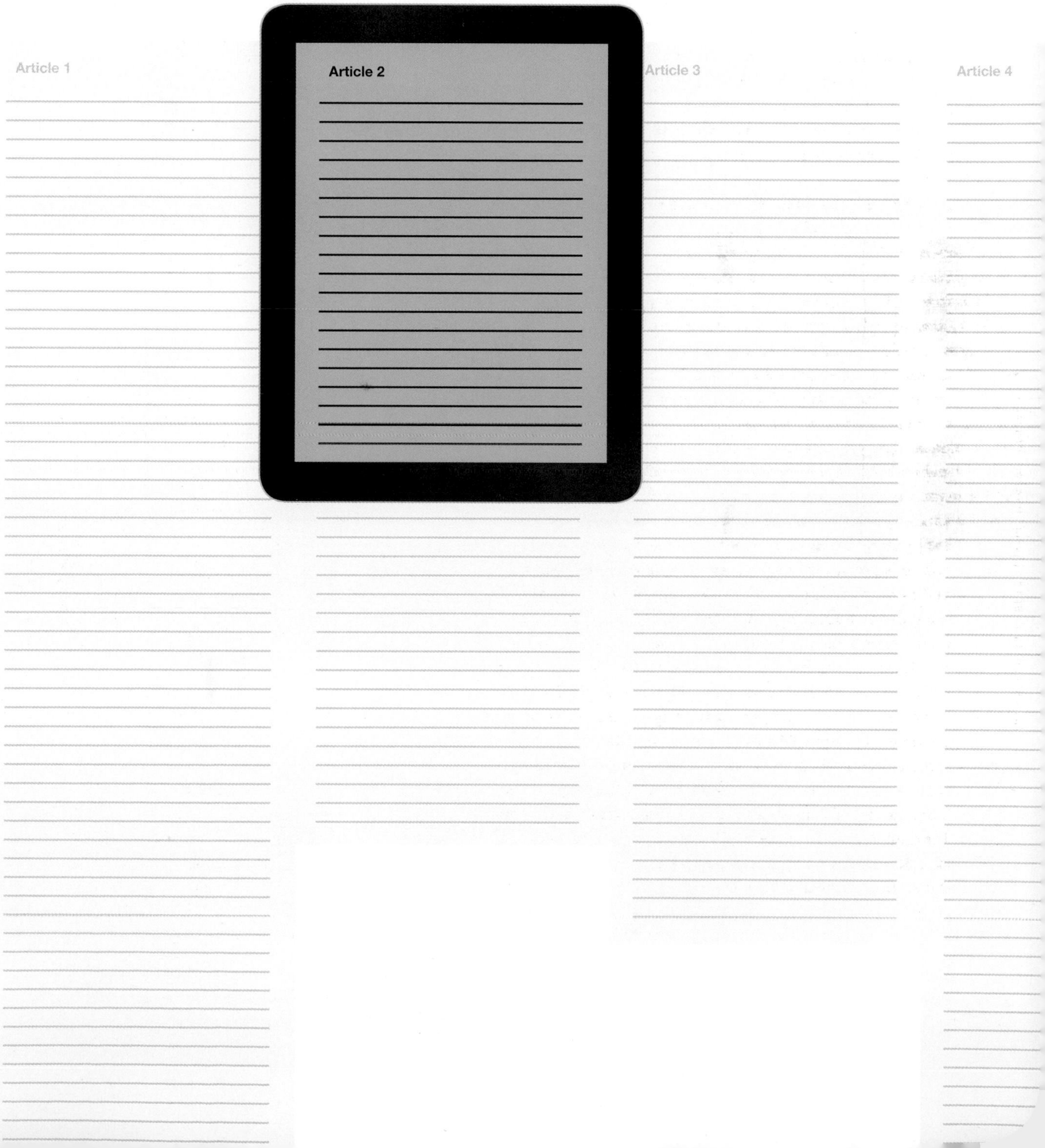

Article 1

Article 2

Article 3

Article 4

Chapter

4 TYPO

GRAPHY

"Typography in practice is not choosing fonts or making fonts, it's about shaping text for optimal user experience."
—OLIVER REICHENSTEIN

115

CORE WEB FONTS FROM LOCAL COMPUTER

1 p { font-family: 'Impact', Arial Black; }

The style sheet calls for a specific font, in this case Impact with Arial Black as the fallback.

2

If Impact is available, the font on the user's computer will be used to render the text.

3

The browser renders text successfully using Impact.

SAFE WEB FONTS ▪ Macintosh and Windows computers come pre-installed with what are called core web fonts or common fonts: typefaces freely available on Macintosh and Windows operating systems, that can also be installed on Linux and Unix systems. A design that calls for a headline to appear in Impact will rely on the Impact font file at the user's local computer to render the headline. However, if a font such as Gotham gets specified, it would only load on a computer that has Gotham in its system fonts. If Gotham is not installed, a fallback font would be used.

Specifying core fonts such as these will ensure that the typography appears the way you want when a website appears on a digital device.

Arial
by Robin Nicholas and Patricia Saunders, 1982

Arial Black
by Robin Nicholas and Patricia Saunders, 1982

Helvetica
by Max Miedinger and Eduard Hoffmann, 1957

Impact
by Geoffrey Lee, 1965

Tahoma
by Matthew Carter and Tom Rickner, 1994

Trebuchet
by Vincent Connare, 1996

Verdana
by Matthew Carter, 1996

Georgia
by Matthew Carter, 1996

Times New Roman
by Stanley Morison and Victor Lardent, 1932

Andale Mono
by Steve Matteson, 1995

Courier New
originally a typewriter face for IBM,
redrawn by Adrian Frutiger,
further developed by Howard Kettler, 1995

GENERIC FONT DICTATED BY USER'S BROWSER

1   p { font-family: sans-serif; }

A style sheet calls for a sans serif, and not a specific font such as Arial or Helvetica.

2

Font Settings for:
Serif: Times
Sans-Serif: Arial

The web browser's preferences determine what font to use when a sans serif gets called for.

3   Arial   →   a

The browser tells the computer to use Arial, and it calls on the font file from the user's computer to render text.

Generic fonts, on the other hand, are part of a web browser's settings. In many cases, a browser has a default setting. But users can tell their browser or email program to make the generic serif face be whatever they want—from Mrs Eaves to Bodoni—so long as that font is loaded on their computer. Using the generic font-family property gives the designer less control over the typography to be displayed, and ultimately puts the user in control of which fonts will appear. Generic font-family properties can be combined with calling core fonts. This will ensure that if one of the specified core fonts is not available, the user's browser will default to a similar-looking font. This would appear as **p { font-family: 'Times New Roman', Times, serif; }** in the CSS attributes; and if neither Times New Roman nor Times was available, then the browser would default to whatever serif face the user has set in her preferences because of the "serif" denotation at the end.

The CSS font-family properties below enable the user's browser to render whatever font they've chosen for each of the five categories. This depreciated font tagging method does not give the designer as much control of how the text content will appear.

SERIF
p { font-family: serif; }

SANS-SERIF
p { font-family: sans-serif; }

Cursive
p { font-family: cursive; }

FANTASY
p { font-family: fantasy; }

MONOSPACE
p { font-family: monospace; }

HOW FONTS GET REFERENCED FROM A THIRD PARTY

A CSS stylesheet, javascript file, or both types of files specify a font for displaying text. Multiple files may exist in the backend, just to ensure that the fonts load properly.

1
```
<link rel="Stylesheet" type="text/css" href="fonts.css" />

<script type="text/javascript" src="fontscript.js"></script>
```

The instructions above tell the browser where to find the font file online so it can be used to render the website's text. The font may exist at the website server a user visits or on a third party server such as Google's or Typekit's.

2 http://cloud-load-font.com/font?family=Skia

External Font File

The server allows the user's computer to render text with the assigned font.

3

Skia → a

But the font only resides on an external server, and not on the user's local computer storage.

4

Skia

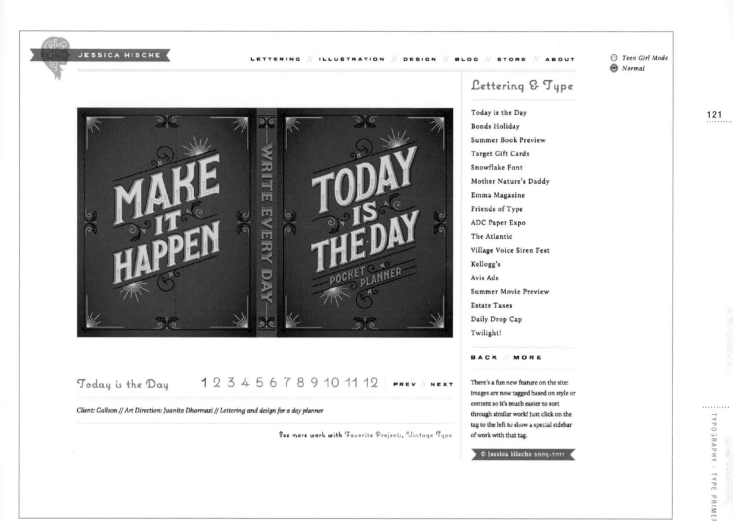

Jessica Hische's website uses Typekit to load fonts from a server-based system. The fonts used in her website's menus, submenus, and footer do not reside locally on a user's computer, but rather on a network-based server and are only rendered on-screen.

REFERENCING/LOADING FONTS ▪ The limitations of generic fonts and core fonts continue to weigh heavily on designers who want to use the breadth of fonts they've grown accustomed to when working in print. Although software and plug-ins, such as Flash, allow almost any font to display on a website, not every device uses Flash or has it enabled. Fortunately, emerging technologies have begun to let designers call upon a library of fonts through services such as Typekit, Google Web Fonts, and WOFF (Web Open Font Format). During a time when cloud computing lets users store documents, photographs, email, and music in a cloud-based server (a storage system that does not reside locally on one's computer hard drive), cloud-based fonts will likely gain momentum too. Through this font cloud method, typefaces would sit on a server or hard drive, and then get displayed on a user's computer.

Permutations and Sizes

As typographers and foundries translate more and more fonts for digital display, using a font may not necessarily mean owning a font. Conventionally, designers, production houses, and service bureaus would pay for a font file that they stored on their computer, along with a license that granted them certain usage rights. Since typographers and foundries now store font files in the cloud with an online service bureau, the file itself does not need to reside on the designers' hard disk.

When selecting a typeface, ask yourself . . .

Does it have a minimum or complete character set?

Are there extended characters?

What about Latin, non-Latin, and Cyrillic?

What about siblings, cousins, and ligatures?

Is there a noticeable difference across weights and styles?

How does the type look across different platforms/devices?

Can contrast make the type readable at all sizes?

Do alternates exist to set fallback fonts?

This poses advantages for both parties, and ultimately benefits the typographers and foundries the most, as they now have better oversight of their products. But with so many fonts available, where does one start? Traditionally, print designers could rely on a handful of favorites that they may have preferred since they knew how the typeface would perform visually. However, since some of those typefaces have been adapted for the screen, subtle changes may have occurred, in effect, changing it visually. Worse yet, some of those favorites may not be available for digital use. A number of questions should be considered before settling on a typeface, one of which includes fallback fonts: If the font you've chosen isn't available, make sure another font that looks somewhat similar can be used instead.

Serif Stack
Minion Pro
Constantia
Hoefler Text
Georgia
Times

Sans Serif Stack
Myriad Pro
Verdana
Helvetica
Arial
Trebuchet

Alternate Sans Serif Stack
Gill Sans
Trebuchet
Helvetica
Arial
Verdana

After making comparisons above, the designer would need to decide if the font in the stack is in fact a good choice. The closer the typefaces look, the better they'll work together in the stack.

With the plethora of digital devices that will continue to increase over time, designers have the added challenge of delivering a design that can adapt from one device to the next. The days of designing for the device seem to be dwindling away, with designers and developers placing a greater emphasis on delivering the content across screens, no matter their size.
Verdana

With the plethora of digital devices that will continue to increase over time, designers have the added challenge of delivering a design that can adapt from one device to the next. The days of designing for the device seem to be dwindling away, with designers and developers placing a greater emphasis on delivering the content across screens, no matter their size.
Georgia

Verdana and Georgia both work well for text type because of their generous counters and spacing.

TYPEFACE COMPARISONS ACROSS A STACK

Prior to 2010, designers had two basic options: Use any of the core web fonts or make the type into an image. Core web fonts gave designers a limited selection of serifs and sans serifs that resided on most users' computer hard disks. This meant only sans serif fonts such as Arial, Helvetica, Tahoma, and Verdana or serifs such as Courier, Georgia, and Times could be loaded into a web page. This made the typeface selection process rather easy, although it did not deliver the range of styles print designers had been accustomed to.

MODE's design for Mellow Mushroom mirrors the pizzeria's fun and frolicking attitude with everything from in-your-face photography to handcrafted cartoonish typography.

1 I l — Verdana

1 I l — Arial

1 I l — Helvetica

Verdana has noticeable differentiation between similar-looking glyphs such as the number 1, capital *I*, and lowercase *l*, whereas Arial and Helvetica have too much similarity.

Sans Serif Type
Verdana

Sans Serif Type
News Gothic MT

Sans Serif Type
Arial

Sans Serif Type
Helvetica

Sans Serif Type
Trebuchet

Sans Serif Type
Tahoma

Sans Serif Type
Gill Sans

A font will often contain a range of styles including bold, italic, wide, narrow, or all-caps derivations. But a font's basis—often referred to as normal or regular—will look light or heavy when compared with another typeface. By setting each of these typefaces in 14-pt. regular, differences in weight and width become evident. The top four faces, Verdana, News Gothic MT, Arial, and Helvetica, all set wider than the others. But News Gothic MT appears lighter, with increased inter-letter spacing. Of them all, Gill Sans sets the narrowest, has the shortest x-height, and would need to be set larger in order to improve readability.

Sans Serif Type
Tahoma

Sans Serif Type
News Gothic MT

Sans Serif Type
Arial

Sans Serif Type
Helvetica

Sans Serif Type
Verdana

Sans Serif Type
Gill Sans

Sans Serif Type
Trebuchet

Sans Serif Type
Gill Sans 16 pt.

When set in 14-pt. boldface, Tahoma appears the heaviest, and 14-pt. Verdana sets the widest. Optically, notice how Gill Sans Bold set at 14 pt. appears very heavy because of the smaller counters. But setting Gill Sans Bold at 16 pt. will make it heavier than Tahoma. Despite these faces being set in simply boldface, many fonts continue to be updated for digital display with a range of weights such as medium, semibold, and black.

Serif Type
Palatino

Serif Type
Georgia

Serif Type
Times

Serif Type
Adobe Caslon Pro

Serif Type
Baskerville

Serif Type
Minion Pro

Serif Type
Book Antiqua

Of the 14 pt.-serifs, Georgia turns out to be the densest in terms of weight, but Palatino sets wider. Baskerville appears lighter in comparison to the others, with Adobe Garamond and Book Antiqua possessing shorter x-heights.

Serif Type
Georgia

Serif Type
Baskerville

Serif Type
Palatino

Serif Type
Times

Serif Type
Minion Pro

Serif Type
Adobe Caslon Pro

Serif Type
Book Antiqua

Georgia is the clear winner in the weight and width category. Palatino has a number of eccentricities that would need to be properly hinted when translated for digital display, such as the elongated serif at the descender of the lowercase *p*. Baskerville—very heavy in its own right—shares that property, but has a much shorter descender distance, and like Georgia, this keeps lines of text from bumping into one another.

Silverpoint's website for the University of Chicago Laboratory Schools possesses a clear hierarchy of information, akin to any newspaper, magazine, brochure, or poster layout: Large features with varying type styles and sizes break content into distinct zones.

Permutations should be done with capital letters in order to see how wide lines will set. Some fonts will contain small caps for special uses.

SERIF TYPOGRAPHY
Palatino

SERIF TYPOGRAPHY
Georgia

SERIF TYPOGRAPHY
Times

SERIF TYPOGRAPHY
Adobe Caslon Pro

SERIF TYPOGRAPHY
Baskerville

SERIF TYPOGRAPHY
Minion Pro

SERIF TYPOGRAPHY
Book Antiqua

Examining numbers will help identify what fonts have lining or nonlining numbers.

0123456789
Palatino

0123456789
Georgia

0123456789
Times

0123456789
Adobe Caslon Pro

0123456789
Baskerville

0123456789
Minion Pro

0123456789
Book Antiqua

A number of methods exist for sizing typography for the screen including points, pixels, ems, and percentages (often denoted by simply %). Points and pixels are absolute measuring devices, and are best suited for layouts that do not change from format to format. Prior to the advent of mobile devices, absolute sizes ensured that the designers' typography would look the same from one browser to another. But as more digital devices come to market, and users learn to change their settings to meet their own needs, relative sizing has gained traction. Relative sizes such as the em and % work best for fluid layouts, where a design exists across a number of platforms such as a desktop, tablet, and mobile phone. Today's hardware and software have text size settings that users can change, and designing with relative sizes allows the type size to meet whatever they've set. The Firefox browser has a default text size of 16 pixels, and sizing type to be 1 em (or the equivalent 100%) means that type would appear as the set 16 pixels. However, if a user has increased the default type size to be 20 pixels, the 1 em setting would make all typography appear at the 20 pixels she prefers. Relative sizing will adapt to the user and the device, but absolute sizing will not. Sizing keywords can also be used, and range from xx-small to xx-large, with varying degrees in between.

Sizing with Ems

1 em = 100% = 16 pixels

1.5 em = 150% = 24 pixels

0.5 em = 50% = 8 pixels

These ratios demonstrate how text sized in ems would scale for somebody using a 16-pixel text size in her application preferences.

1 em = 100% = 20 pixels

1.5 em = 150% = 30 pixels

0.50 em = 50% = 10 pixels

However, if a user preferred a larger text size, and set her software to display text at 20 pixels, type would get sized much differently.

An image-heavy layout like this site by Social Design House uses typographic hierarchy between the menu, artwork title, and subnavigation.

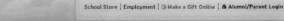

Giving Overview

A strong tradition of philanthropy stretches back to the earliest days at Asheville School.

The continued support of the school's alumni and friends has been the difference between a good school and a great school, between moving forward or remaining static.

There are many ways to show support for Asheville School, whether giving to the institution's annual, capital or estate giving funds, or volunteering for one of many on- or off-campus events.

The giving will be appreciated by the administration, faculty and students for generations to come.

Procedures for stock transfers:

The simplest (and fastest) way to transmit stock is for your broker to do a DTC transfer through one of the school's brokers:

Van Thompson (Class of '73) of Morgan Keegan in Lexington, KY
859.253.9769 (phone) van.thompson@morgankeegan.com (email)

Your broker will need the following information:
Our DTC Number: 780
The account of Asheville School: 270–55896

---OR---

Bob Anning (Class of '59) of Merrill Lynch in Cincinnatti, OH
1.800.234.2099 (phone)

Your broker will need the following information:
Our DTC number: 5198
The account of Asheville School: 636–04482

We like to call our broker to ask that they be on the lookout for all transfers. If you can provide the security being transferred in advance to the School (and the number of shares, or the approximate amount), it is easier for our broker to track the gift.

School Tax ID#: 56–0530248

> I talk to my classmates on a weekly basis, and we are all nostalgic about Asheville School. I feel very confident in saying that Asheville School was the best four years of my life so far. All the memories are so vivid; it's a special place.

Gary J. Shields, Class of 2002
Los Angeles, California
University of Southern California
Grad School, Music Composition

One of the key factors in typographic design is hierarchy: creating noticeable levels of difference between information to help readers identify primary, secondary, and tertiary content. This interface by Silverpoint uses varying type styles, type sizes, positions, and colors in order to guide readers from one zone to the next. Even little details like a large blue quotation mark tell the user what she's about to read.

Designing with Type

TEXT TYPE ■ Typefaces such as Caslon, Baskerville, Bembo, and Georgia were designed for text, paragraph, or book type. When set in long forms, they make uninterrupted reading easy for the user. Oftentimes text type works well when set in small or large sizes. The readily available Georgia was designed to function well on-screen for long-form reading, and makes an adequate choice for laying out digital books. Clearface, Centaur, and Sabon also have good readability. Line length, word spacing, and leading all factor into a book text's readability, but choosing a time-tested typeface such as those listed in this chapter is as good a place as any to start. And while some print designers come from a tradition of using serifs predominantly for text type, sans serifs and slab serifs work well on-screen because they are not as noisy as some serifs.

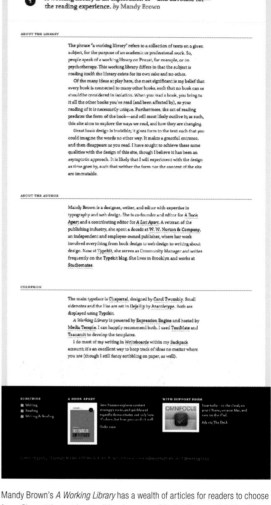

Studiobanks used a simple sans serif that reads crisply when set as text type. To create differentiation among the typographic layout, a compressed face was used for the top-navigation items.

Mandy Brown's *A Working Library* has a wealth of articles for readers to choose from. She set the text in a traditional manner of flush left, ragged right, with paragraphs denoted by indentations. Even the links appear subtly underlined as dashes, so as not to interrupt the reader's flow.

DISPLAY TYPE ▪ Like messages on posters, advertisements, and promotions, display type needs to catch readers' attention. Setting type in a larger size is one way to achieve this effect, but using a typeface intended for a headline and subhead speaks to readers more distinctly. Slab serifs such as Rockwell, Memphis, and Clarendon have enough of the weight and uniqueness necessary to lure readers in. Finally, a variety of sans serifs and scripts can also do the job well.

In this image-heavy layout by version industries (v), a limited sans serif palette has been used for menus and captions. Setting menu items in all caps and captions in sentence case creates just enough differentiation between the content areas.

Firebelly set each of the arts disciplines in a large sans serif face, even continuing the words over the column edge to the next line. The effect makes readers flow from one line to the next, while maintaining readability.

Method's design for the Teaching Channel uses display type large enough to capture your attention, such as the "When does 1+1+1=$10?" callout with its "Find out" call to action.

TYPE FOR NAVIGATION ▪ A benefit to the digital domain is its depth: We can navigate through a morass of content quickly and easily by typing in an address. At our destination, we can click icon-based buttons or text-based links to go well beyond the place we landed. And until voice recognition becomes fully supported, we will continue to rely on buttons and links to take us from one place to another. Conventions helped users in the 1990s move around from site to site. At that time, underlines signified an active link, that would jump you to another portion of the site, an alternate area on the same page, or a completely different website altogether. Those conventions continue to be used today, but many liberties are taken with type used for navigation, be it as a menu or hyperlink.

Eric Karjaluoto of smashLAB explains the benefits of conventions: "Imagine going to pick up your toothbrush, only to find a shovel in its place; or stepping on your car's accelerator, only to find it replaced with the brake pedal. Conventions are necessary for one simple reason: Once we learn where something is—and how it works—we don't want someone going in and messing with it. The fact is that websites are going to change a great deal in the next few years. The biggest driver of this is the multitude of devices that need to access the same data/content—be it on your laptop, mobile phone, touchscreen, or tablet, new conventions will start to emerge that better bridge the mouse/finger barrier." When designers began using CSS to change text styling, they did away with certain conventions. One of them included doing away with the underline that signified hyperlinked text. Instead, they would change the type color or background, or leave it completely unstylized. This created a lot of commotion among some users, because a change had happened, and it was one they were not necessarily prepared for.

Conventional and colorful, Paul Soulellis set active links with underlines in a light shade of blue to give users what they're used to, and connect the link color to the NewTalk identity.

When we're reading text and we want to know exactly where the <u>hyperlinks</u> are, most of us don't want to work too hard. We want to get an immediate cue that tells us exactly where <u>to click</u>. Although <u>some experts</u> suggest that all hyperlinked or type-based navigation should have an underline to signify it's an active link, that practice is becoming less of a convention.

Underlines have been a standard convention to help users identify hyperlinks, and make it easy to find links in text.

When we're reading text and we want to know exactly where the <u>hyperlinks</u> are, most of us don't want to work too hard. We want to get an immediate cue that tells us exactly where <u>to click</u>. Although <u>some experts</u> suggest that all hyperlinked or type-based navigation should have an underline to signify it's an active link, that practice is becoming less of a convention.

Dashed underlines elicit a subtler amount of differentiation.

When we're reading text and we want to know exactly where the *hyperlinks* are, most of us don't want to work too hard. We want to get an immediate cue that tells us exactly where *to click*. Although *some books*, such as User Interface Guidelines, Rules, and Protocols, suggest that all hyperlinked or type-based navigation should have an underline to signify it's an active link, that practice is becoming less of a convention.

Italic type works just as well, but trouble may arise if books, magazines, or movies are in the text. In those cases, making the italic links a different color will improve differentiation.

Ultranoir's design for Kididoc delivers a typographic treasure trove of styles, appropriate given the content and audience. Different typefaces, styles, and buttons delineate various links.

Studiobanks set menu typography for the Varji & Varji site in all caps and bolded the visitor's current location to help them identify where they are in the site.

When we're reading text and we want to know exactly where the **hyperlinks** are, most of us don't want to work too hard. We want to get an immediate cue that tells us exactly where **to click**. Although **some experts** suggest that all hyperlinked or type-based navigation should have an underline to signify it's an active link, that practice is becoming less of a convention.

Bolds will help call out links with plenty of emphasis.

When we're reading text and we want to know exactly where the hyperlinks are, most of us don't want to work too hard. We want to get an immediate cue that tells us exactly where to click. Although some experts suggest that all hyperlinked or type-based navigation should have an underline to signify it's an active link, that practice is becoming less of a convention.

Reversing the text creates an even heavier break between the links and body text, and looks too loud.

When we're reading text and we want to know exactly where the hyperlinks are, most of us don't want to work too hard. We want to get an immediate cue that tells us exactly where to click. Although some experts suggest that all hyperlinked or type-based navigation should have an underline to signify it's an active link, that practice is becoming less of a convention.

Setting a background color behind the text creates a balance between the body text and highlighted links.

By setting the headline WE'RE TWOFOLD and the caption beneath it flush right, the left edge conforms naturally to the child's silhouette. This is a case where Twofold Creative looked carefully at composition to decide text setting, to ensure the image and type work well together.

Silverpoint used a predominantly flush-left setting for the text in this site.

Landers Miller Design created a typographically rich interface for the Sweetery NYC mobile food truck. The wealth of typographic alignments, styles, and sizes mimics the plethora of flavors that the Sweetery brings to its customers.

The Schottenstein Center website places the brand identity in the
centermost position of the header, giving it prominence and focus.

When version industries (v) set text for the Beyond Apollo site, the effect is one of order and
cleanliness, with paragraph edges looking clean and straight. But use caution, since justified
text settings often have open spaces that connect vertically across paragraph lines, called rivers.

Running Text. As in the printed world, pull quotes alert readers that something important exists within the article, and pulls them in to read the entire text. Jason Santa Maria put these and other typographic niceties throughout the site.

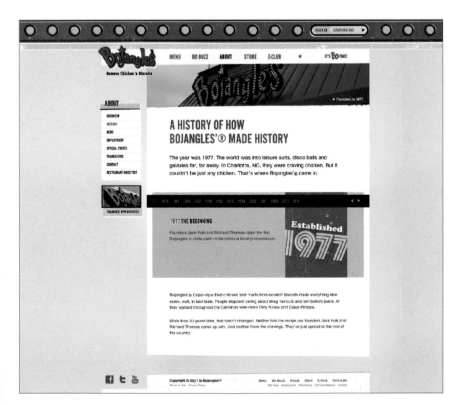

Footers. When Sparkbox designed the footer for their online presence, they decided to have a little fun by creating three footer options for readers: standard, impressive, and feva.

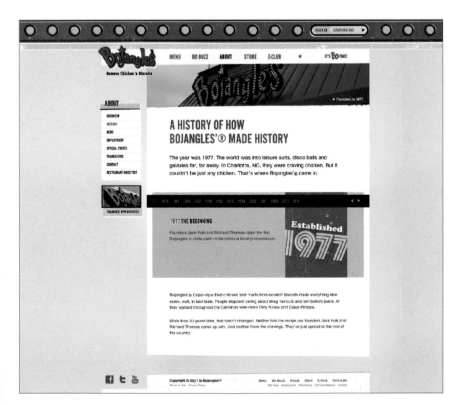

Headlines. Setting a headline in a big, bold display face doesn't require the text to be set in black. A site by Studiobanks keys the large headline off the red in the brand identity and photograph. And the Established 1977 callout appears in a different typeface and size altogether.

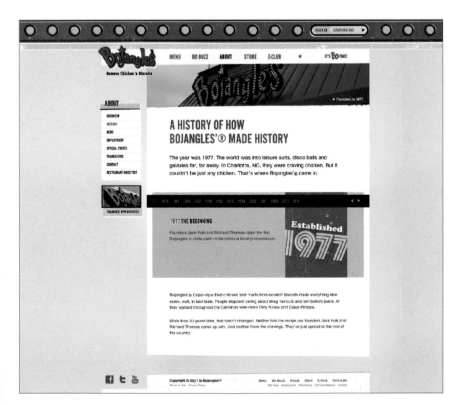

Art Criticism and Writing | MFA Program

S·V·A School of VISUAL ARTS

home
program
faculty
news and events
lecture series
admissions
contact us
degree critical blog

search

KEEP IN TOUCH

Follow us on Facebook
Subscribe to our RSS Feed
Join our Mailing List

MFA Art Criticism & Writing
School of Visual Arts
209 E. 23 Street, 7th Floor
New York, NY 10010
212.592.2408
artcrit@sva.edu

WHAT'S NEW:

Fall 2011 Enrollment Date Extended!
We are now accpting applications for Fall 2011 enrollment up to July 15.
Learn more about our application process and requirements, click here.

VISIT THE DEGREE CRITICAL BLOG

Degree Critical is our student run blog featuring reviews and critiques from exhibits and shows in New York.

OUR MISSION:

The MFA program in Art Criticism & Writing is one of the only graduate writing programs in the world that focuses specifically on criticism. This program is not involved in "discourse production" or the prevarications of curatorial rhetoric, but rather in the practice of criticism writ large, aspiring to literature.

MEET THE FACULTY

Suzanne Anker:
Chair, BFA Fine Arts Department, School of Visual Arts; fine artist; critic. Learn more

View all Faculty

FROM OUR LECTURE SERIES

LUCY LIPPARD
Ghosts, the Daily News, and Prophecy: Critical Landscape Photography.

View Video

LATEST NEWS:

Miriam Atkin (class of 2010) and Kurt Ralske (class of 2012) at Location One, April 27th. Rediscovering German Futurist Cinema, 1920-1929

View All News

WE'RE READING

Adorno Philosophy Of New Music
Theodor W. Adorno (Author)

View all Books

The Latest from Degree Critical Blog

Between Life & Death, Or Between Sea and Land
by Nayun Lee

Dominique Gonzalez-Foerster, "T.1912" at the Solomon R. Guggenheim Museum, NY, August 14, 2011

The French artist Dominique Gonzalez-Foerster turned the Guggenheim Museum into a sinking Titanic on the evening of April 14th. The day was the 99th anniversary of the tragedy, which took 1,517 lives. "T.1912" was a site-specific performance, which was perfectly synchronized with the museum's structure, and included the Wordless Music Orchestra, lighting and audience participation

Continue Reading

Share + | Permalink

MFA Art Criticism and Writing
©School of Visual Arts

209 E. 23 Street,
7th Floor
New York, NY 10010
212.592.2408
artcrit@sva.edu

Home
Program
Faculty
News and Events
Lecture Series

Admissions
Degree Critical Blog
Contact

A text-heavy site like the School of Visual Arts' MFA Art Criticism and Writing requires headlines, subheads, and body text, and also captions to address imagery. Landers Miller Design even gave links a distinct treatment to help readers discern between where to click and where to read.

Promoting a band requires a wealth of media to be displayed online, including social media feeds, vlogs (video blogs), and shopping cards. A sans serif and slab serif do most of the heavy lifting, and as an added bonus, members of the Gregory Brothers speak thanks to the typographic speech bubbles version industries (v) imposes as pop ups.

The rule of noticeable differences is as relevant to sizing type as it is to pairing type. If differentiation must happen between levels of information so that a hierarchy is evident, noticeably different sizes should be used. Setting items in the same typeface, where a headline is 16 pixels and a subhead in 15 pixels, does little to differentiate the two. Use a mathematical multiplier—also called a matrix—to help create size stacks, or areas for placing visual elements. Mathematical proportions rely on numerical relationships. The Fibonacci sequence is one example of an integer sequence where subsequent numbers get added to the preceding one: 0, 1, 1, 2, 3, 5, 8, 13, 21, and to get the next number in the series, add 13 to 21 to get 34. Multiples of two, three, or four can also be used, with multiples of four coming in handy when establishing leading and line height.

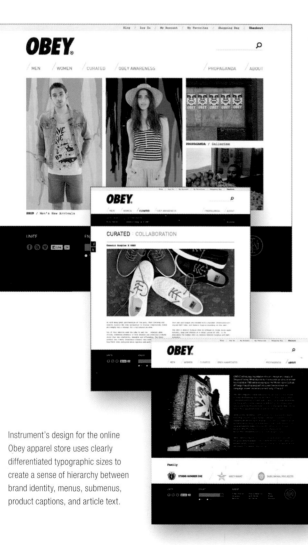

Instrument's design for the online Obey apparel store uses clearly differentiated typographic sizes to create a sense of hierarchy between brand identity, menus, submenus, product captions, and article text.

Scaling type sizes by Fibonacci

Headline
34 point

Subhead
21 point

Pull Quote
13 point italic

Body Text
13 point

Caption
8 point

Scaling type sizes by factor of four

Headline
24 points

Subhead
20 points

Pull Quote
16 point—italic

Body Text
12 point

Caption
8 point

Scaling type sizes by factor of three

Headline
21 points

Subhead
18 point

Pull Quote
15 point

Body Text
12 point

Caption
9 point

Ultranoir used typefaces with nostalgic flair to bring the site's viewers back to the roaring 1920s and turbulent 1930s. Large headlines pull readers in, with smaller body text giving more backstory.

Nuances

LEADING AND SPACING ■ The space between lines of typography has been called leading, inter-line spacing, and line height. At present, design software typically sets type with 120 percent leading, making a 12-point font have 14.4 points of leading. But that is not the ideal calculation. For improved readability, set the typography in the necessary size, measure the space between each word, and add that measurement (or more) to the type size for your leading. In the digital realm, many of us experience type in the default manner in which our software or hardware goes about rendering it. Phones and tablets have limited typographic capabilities, and some of the software lets us customize type styles and sizes, but few products let us change leading. Although there are settings to customize typography, and in some cases the leading, it's rare that we do so for the casual communication we send. But that may soon change. What many of us deem primitive—the typewriter—evolved into typesetting, desktop publishing, word processing, and then design software. Already, ereaders such as Amazon's Kindle and Barnes & Noble's Nook let users customize typefaces and leading. In time, we may see other digital devices let us adjust typefaces and leading to our preferences.

In this text-heavy layout, MODE established a top-down sense of hierarchy; with the feature text set larger and tertiary items set smaller. Noticeable headlines over each article give readers cues about the material, and also work well with search engines.

A designer's job will become even more challenging as the quantity of information and noise increases during the twenty-first century. Designers who possess a broad typographic understanding will best meet the communicative and creative challenge, especially during a time when people know the difference between one font or another— and which ones read better or worse with software's default typographic leading.

Setting text at 12 points with 16 points of inter-line spacing yields an open enough body of text to be readable.

A designer's job will become even more challenging as the quantity of information and noise increases during the twenty-first century. Designers who possess a broad typographic understanding will best meet the communicative and creative challenge, especially during a time when people know the difference between one font or another— and which ones read better or worse with software's default typographic leading.

Now with 18 points of leading, more air exists between the text.

A designer's job will become even more challenging as the quantity of information and noise increases during the twenty-first century. Designers who possess a broad typographic understanding will best meet the communicative and creative challenge, especially during a time when people know the difference between one font or another— and which ones read better or worse with software's default typographic leading.

Anything greater than 160 percent leading, in this case a 12-point font with 20 points of leading, will deliver plenty of inter-line spacing for the reader. But use care when doing so, as the text will take up more space.

Home

Columns

Articles

Biographies

Ordering

Help

Baseline Alignment. A baseline grid that runs across separate columns of text will establish cross-alignment and a vertical rhythm. In this case, both columns have been set with 20 points of leading to foster the relationship.

Western cultures, especially those based on Romantic languages, have been known to align typography using a flush-left—also called ranged-left or ragged-right—setting because it lets readers, who move from left to right, find the next line in a text measure without much trouble. This is not the norm in languages that have alternate reading directions, such as Arabic, Hebrew, and Japanese. At one time, the Greeks had text settings that began with left to right reading, and forced the reader to continue on the next line down in the opposite direction, from right to left. Some conventions require designers to lay out text in flush-left, flush-right, or centered settings. This becomes more about values, attitudes, and traditions that dictate what the norm is. Customarily, wedding invitations use center alignment to place the names of the couple and their designated families in the middle of the format, making it easy to find out who's who.

Home

Columns

Articles

Biographies

Ordering

Help

Even with a larger 24-point leading in the left menu column and the same 20-point leading in the right, both columns will align sporadically because of the factor of four used.

Western cultures, especially those based on Romantic languages, have been known to align typography using a flush-left—also called ranged-left or ragged-right—setting because it lets readers, who move from left to right, find the next line in a text measure without much trouble. This is not the norm in languages that have alternate reading directions, such as Arabic, Hebrew, and Japanese. At one time, the Greeks had text settings that began with left to right reading, and forced the reader to continue on the next line down in the opposite direction, from right to left. Some conventions require designers to lay out text in flush-left, flush-right, or centered settings. This becomes more about values, attitudes, and traditions that dictate what the norm is. Customarily, wedding invitations use center alignment to place the names of the couple and their designated families in the middle of the format, making it easy to find out who's who.

THE PARAGRAPH ▪ Differentiating paragraphs helps readers distinguish between one idea and the next when they are reading a large body of information. Paragraph designators include, but are not limited to, breaks, indentations, markers, or a combination thereof. New paragraphs can happen through a direct and abrupt separation.

Tabs are another convention that is recognizable and acceptable, but not always easy to achieve in the digital realm, least of all when typing an email. In email, it's become customary to place two hard returns after a paragraph for separation, but digitally composing with HTML or CSS lets designers adjust leading and paragraph spacing with greater control.

Mandy Brown's site uses tabs to delineate paragraphs and hard returns to separate sections.

Traditional designers, who work predominantly in printed media, know the specifics of building a document that's press ready, specifying the right paper, getting bids on a job, and seeing the design through the printing and delivery process. Electronic media has its own final production process with checkpoints in place to meet the end goal.

The five key checkpoints, in addition to visual design, include implementation, testing, documentation, launch, and maintenance. During implementation, developers program the site so that it functions. Testing investigates how the site operates on browsers and the ways users interact with it. Documentation collects all of that information and analyzes it in order to aid in the launch and maintenance.

Paragraphs separated by two hard returns with 12 points of leading between them.

Traditional designers, who work predominantly in printed media, know the specifics of building a document that's press ready, specifying the right paper, getting bids on a job, and seeing the design through the printing and delivery process. Electronic media has its own final production process with checkpoints in place to meet the end goal.

The five key checkpoints, in addition to visual design, include implementation, testing, documentation, launch, and maintenance. During implementation, developers program the site so that it functions. Testing investigates how the site operates on browsers and the ways users interact with it. Documentation collects all of that information and analyzes it in order to aid in the launch and maintenance.

In this case, the line height between paragraphs has been adjusted, and rather than a full slot of leading, one-half its size has been used. While these breaks are subtler, and often used in book texts, they can create problems when cross-aligning columns.

Traditional designers, who work predominantly in printed media, know the specifics of building a document that's press ready, specifying the right paper, getting bids on a job, and seeing the design through the printing and delivery process. Digital media has its own final production process with checkpoints in place to meet the end goal. ¶ The five key checkpoints, in addition to visual design, include implementation, testing, documentation, launch, and maintenance. During implementation, developers program the site so that it functions. Testing investigates how the site operates on browsers and the ways users interact with it. Documentation collects all of that information and analyzes it in order to aid in the launch and maintenance.

A paragraph marker (pilcrow) is placed within the text body to maintain the overall flow.

Traditional designers, who work predominantly in printed media, know the specifics of building a document that's press ready, specifying the right paper, getting bids on a job, and seeing the design through the printing and delivery process. Digital media has its own final production process with checkpoints in place to meet the end goal. // The five key checkpoints, in addition to visual design, include implementation, testing, documentation, launch, and maintenance. During implementation, developers program the site so that it functions. Testing investigates how the site operates on browsers and the ways users interact with it. Documentation collects all of that information and analyzes it in order to aid in the launch and maintenance.

These forward slashes do the same job, but are much quieter because the stroke weight matches the font. Other glyphs would achieve the same purpose.

Traditional designers, who work predominantly in printed media, know the specifics of building a document that's press ready, specifying the right paper, getting bids on a job, and seeing the design through the printing and delivery process. Electronic media has its own final production process with checkpoints in place to meet the end goal.

    The five key checkpoints, in addition to visual design, include implementation, testing, documentation, launch, and maintenance. During implementation, developers program the site so that it functions. Testing investigates how the site operates on browsers and the ways users interact with it. Documentation collects all of that information and analyzes it in order to aid in the launch and maintenance.

A tab separates the paragraphs.

FINE DETAILS ▪ One of the more common digital typography mistakes happens when a hyphen is used incorrectly, such as substituting it for an en or em dash. Using a hyphen or hyphens in place of en or em dashes is considered a faux pas. This mistake happens because typing an en or em dash is not as simple as hitting the proper keyboard combination and being done. And those of us used to typing two hyphens together to arrive at an em dash, such as Microsoft Word allows, are at a disadvantage. That trick doesn't work in the online world of typing emails, posting to Twitter, or building an HTML web page.

— em dash

In a typeface's glyph set, the em dash originally referred to the width of the typeface's uppercase M, but today it equals the size of the typeface: 12 pt. type would have a 12 pt. em and 13 pt. type would have a 13 pt. em, and so forth. However, an em dash should not be confused with the em unit of measurement that denotes percentages.

– en dash

An en equals one-half the em dash: 12 pt. type has a 6 pt. en and 13 pt. type would have a 6.5 pt. en.

- hyphen

In the glyph palette, a hyphen is shorter than an en dash.

An em dash—which is long—is often used for a break in thought. It can also — depending on the style — have spaces before and after it.

An en dash can be used to denote distances or ranges such as Barcelona–Madrid, 100–224 km, 1990–92, March–July, or 1:00–2:45 p.m. It is also ideal for open compound words such as the Northern Greece–Albania border.

An en dash also denotes when certain letters have been omitted for reasons of censorship or anonymity, such as Ian Sm – – berg.

fi fl ff ffi ffj

ffl ct st Th

æ Æ Œ œ

When two or more characters conjoin, they are known as a ligature. Traditional typography for print production has enabled ligature control through PostScript, TrueType, and OpenType fonts. OpenType allows ligatures to automatically appear if a ligature is available for a given set of letters. In the digital realm, setting ligatures is not as easy as switching a button. Not all browsers handle ligatures the same, and those that do require backend scripts in order to enable ligatures to appear.

Primes and quotes often get used interchangeably, especially since single and double quotes require a special character code to render using HTML.

| Prime | Single Quote | Double Prime | Double Quote |

He said, 'A single quote is used for citations and quotes in UK English.'

"But in the United States, double quotes are used for quotations," I replied, "and single quotes are used for contractions such as don't or aren't."

When primes get used in the place of quotes, designers often call these *dumb quotes*, because they're not proper. Primes are solely intended for measurement: single prime for feet and minutes, double prime for inches and seconds.

CHUNKING INFORMATION The digital domain offers a wealth of possibilities for delivering typographic content: entire books, magazine and news articles, as well as shorter blog posts, status updates, and microblogs such as Twitter. Behind every piece of content lies a purpose: to chronicle, inform, entertain, advertise, sell, or share. The text should be written and composed in order to fulfill that purpose, and chunking it into small, easily digestible bites lets readers get information one piece at a time.

As a section opener for this book, this text covers a number of issues that a print designer would find valuable. But how do you convert this body text into something scannable? And what about making it into a succinct lead-in that would appear at an online news blog?

A surprising number of graphic designers avoid designing for the web because they fear the production and programming work (the backend). This happens because they think too far ahead, something designers do very well in most cases, in order to understand the short- and long-term issues related to problem solving. Designers will likely look forward to producing the website and all the technical things that go into that construction. Instinctively, they'll consider who will take on the difficult task of doing the backend development and programming. Next, they'll think about what limitations that process may put on their creative direction. A vicious cycle happens where the designer goes back and forth between *I don't understand what goes into a web design project on the backend* and *Since I don't know that backend, there's no way for me to know how to do the frontend design correctly*. In the end, she'll give up on the idea of taking on said project because she cannot address either of those issues.

This original text is rather lengthy, and while it contains a lot of strong points, if it were used as lead-in text on a website some users may not take the time to completely read it.

Graphic designers avoid designing for the web because they fear the production and programming work:

- They think too far ahead.
- They look forward to producing the website.
- They worry too much about how to build it.

Next, they'll think about what limitations that process may put on their creative direction and design:

- I don't understand what goes into a web design project on the backend.
- Since I don't know that backend, there's no way for me to know how to do the frontend design correctly.
- In the end, they'll give up on the idea of taking on said project because they cannot address either of those issues.

Here, the text has been chunked into two sections with bullet points to call out key information.

Graphic designers avoid designing for the web because:

- They think too far ahead.
- They look forward to producing the website.
- They then worry too much about how to program it.

Next, they'll think about what limitations that process may put on their creative direction and design:

- I don't understand how to build it, so there's no way to know how to do the frontend design correctly.
- In the end, they'll give up on said project.

Graphic designers avoid designing for the web because:

- They think too far ahead.
- They look forward to producing the website.
- They then worry too much about how to program it.

Instead, they should realize that they possess the visual literacy and design acumen to properly sketch, plan, and lay out the design.

Graphic designers avoid designing for the web because:

- They think too far ahead.
- They look forward to producing the website.
- They then worry too much about how to program it.

Knowing the backend isn't necessary. Digital design, like print design, can rely on third-party fulfillment.

Graphic designers who avoid designing for the web should realize that, like print design, they rely on third-party fulfillment.

Print designers can capably design for digital media; they just need to apply the principles they already know to the web.

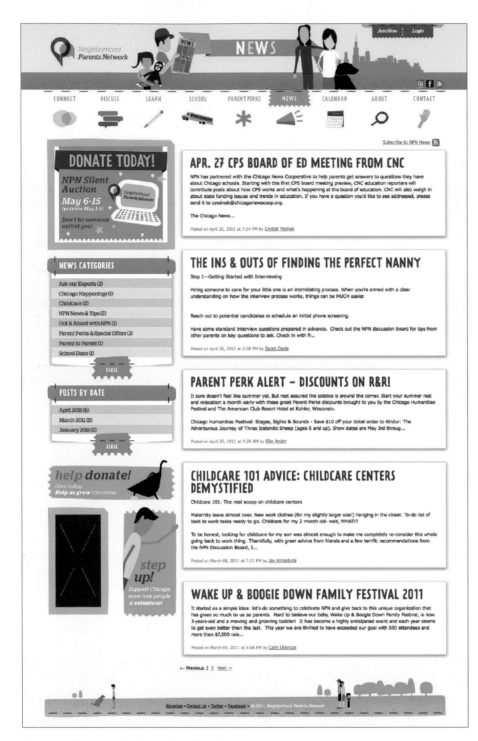

Color, size, position, and copy length all work hand-in-hand to create hierarchy in Firebelly's layout for the Neighborhood Parents Network.

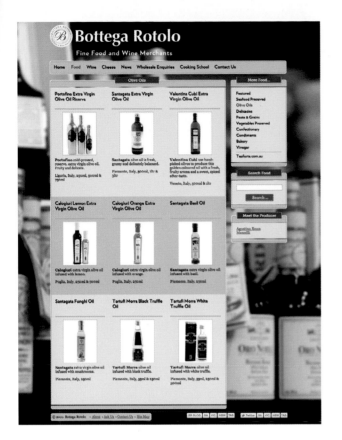

Sometimes you can fit the copy into a layout based on the grid modules. Social Design House used a succinct method of titling each of Coogan's Landscape Design services, with each bit of copy fitting within the image width.

For this layout by Voice, each short bit of copy under a product image tells the reader just enough to get her interested in learning more.

Mobile devices have a smaller screen space, and as such, the copy has to be short and to the point, as illustrated in these Bojangles interfaces by Studiobanks. And since mobile users are often on the go, they don't have the time to sit back and read lengthy material.

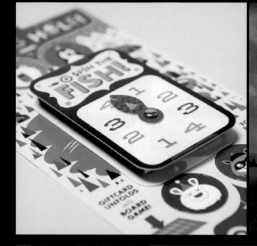

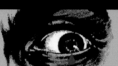

IC + Nike Asia Pacific

When Nike called upon IC to bring some color to their eastern retail, we hit the ground running.

Target House Carnivals

Target House celebrates 10 years and IC is invited . to decorate

IC 'Dead People' + Nonsek

Add ingredients. Stir. Repeat. Our Nonsek Artist Channel is now open for business.

New Invisible Creature Prints

Our new prints await vacant frames across the globe - and just in time for the holidays.

LATEST BLOG POSTS

Happy 2010

Spin The Stork Gift...

Thank You!

Isle Of This Town &...

TWITTERSPHERE

http://twitpic.com/wdkfx - Love this new Jay-Z video! Featuring our

Cool Jonathan Segal Do
http://bit.ly/6gTSYG

@jpidgeon Hey, thanks!

FLICKR

CONTACT

Invisible Creature, Inc.

Instrument's design for Invisible Creature gives small thumbnails for browsing work with small text descriptions to inform readers about the projects.

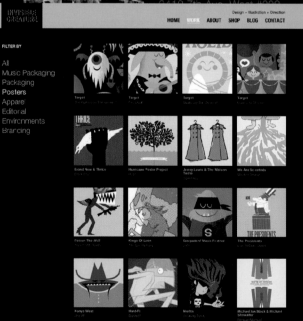

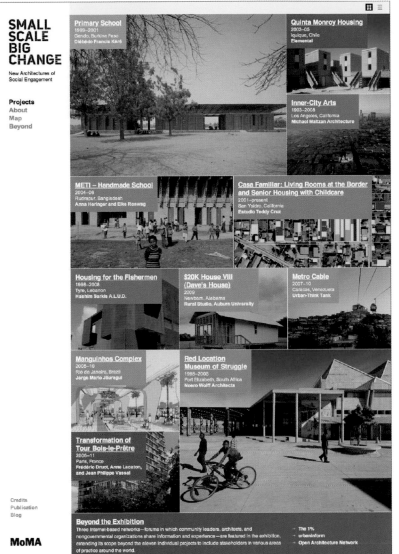

When Method designed MOMA's Small Scale, Big Change: New Architectures of Social Engagement, they used a grid of images as a tool for presenting several items at once. At the browsing level, users view all projects at once for scanning.

Mobile devices have a smaller viewing area, and as such, smaller space for image and text. Ultranoir designed the BVA interface with just enough text to get users where they needed to go in order to complete their transactions.

PAIRING ▪ New challenges have arisen now that more typefaces are available for use, notably pairing. Prior to the web typography revolution, type pairing was as easy as combining Georgia or Times with Arial, Helvetica, Tahoma, Trebuchet, or Verdana. Now there are dozens, if not thousands, of typefaces to choose from. A principal issue that gets overlooked when pairing fonts is contrast: Make sure the typefaces are noticeably different. If you were to combine Times and Garamond, the two serif faces are so similar that no differentiation would be evident. However, if you were to combine the serif Times with a slab serif such as Clarendon or Rockwell, the two are different enough to create a sense of contrast. Moreover, they also have a different weight. Words set in Times will appear lighter than those set in Clarendon.

Other combinations would include pairing a slab serif with a sans serif, script with sans serif, or sans serif with serif. Using a heavier typeface as a headline or subhead will help create a sense of focus. The text could even be set in a different case, either all caps or small caps, to create further differentiation. If you are limited to one font and need to create typographic variety, consider how many variants the font has. A face like Myriad Pro includes Roman, bold, condensed, and italic styles of each of the preceding three. With Myriad Pro alone, a designer could create enough differentiation to lay out an entire book that would include headlines, subheads, body text, captions, and footnotes. Myriad Pro is just one of the many fonts that have this breadth. With the right amount of control and restraint, you can set a layout in more than two typefaces, provided you spread the differentiation around the document. Whether you follow this principle or any other, keep the golden rule in mind: Make things noticeably different. And despite aphorisms such as "Never combine more than two typefaces," do enough visual research and comparison before you make that ideal one of your own.

Two different sans serifs come together successfully in this calendar by Firebelly, thanks to differences in color, size, and weight. Menus, headlines, subheads, lead-ins, and captions all possess their own unique properties.

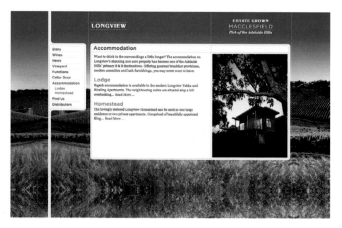

Voice paired a serif in the body text with a sans serif for menus and headers. And above all, the Longview wordmark set in Korinna stands out from those two typefaces as a slab serif.

lazy dog
lazy dog

The serif faces Times (top) and Garamond (bottom) are so similar that using them in a sentence won't achieve the needed contrast, as in the case of lazy dog set in Times.

Slab Serif. A slab juxtaposes nicely next to a serif, provided the serif is lighter in weight.

Slab Serif. Slabs will also work well near sans serifs.

2012 **Slab Serif.** In this case, an ultra light mixes with a slab, and then this light weight.

Slab serifs work well when paired with either serifs or sans serifs. A key factor to look out for is contrast.

Modern No. 20

Setting a narrow face like Helvetica Condensed against a wider, thinly serifed Modern No. 20 provides a sublte amount of differentiation.

Modern No. 20

These two fonts work well when there's a significant difference in the size, and as smaller body text, Helvetica Condensed does the job. Oftentimes, a font pairing will happen best if enough comparison happens. Look at not only the two different typefaces, but also how changes in size, width, weight, or all of the above could help.

You can even pair up two narrow fonts, provided that readers will be able to make sense of the hierarchy.

Preview Day. Welcome to the annual preview day at rockpaperink.com.

Preview Day. Welcome to the annual preview day at rockpaperink.com.

PREVIEW DAY. Welcome to the annual preview day at rockpaperink.com.

PREVIEW DAY. Welcome to the annual preview day at rockpaperink.com.

Helvetica Neue and Minion Pro have enough noticeable differences for them to work well together. The topmost setting has both faces set in the same size and is a less-than-ideal setting. However, the second example from the top has the lowercase x-heights matched up, although *Preview Day*'s uppercase letters appear too small. Lastly, expanded tracking sets off *PREVIEW DAY* even more.

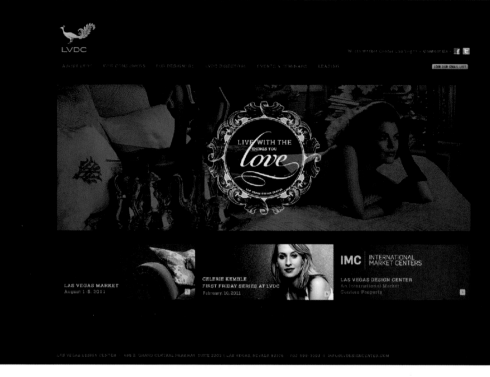

For the Las Vegas Design Center, MODE unified a decorative script in the interface centerpiece, slab serifs for the navigation, a sans serif wordmark, and sans serif footer. Including the IMC wordmark in the bottom right and Facebook and Twitter buttons at the top, this amounts to seven different type treatments.

MODE's award-winning site for Mellow Mushroom Pizza Bakers paired the handcrafted Bad Manners script with slab serif and serif faces. The chunky qualities of Bad Manners work well paired with the sturdy slab serif in the top navigation and Munchies menu.

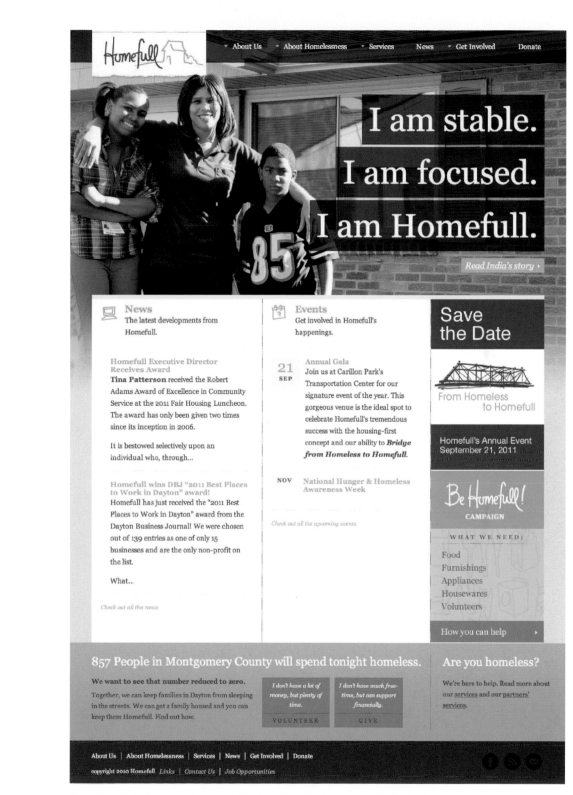

The script used in the Homefull wordmark and Be Homefull! call to action stands out from all of the other typography, creating a clear identity for the organization. Hand-drawn icons and images mirror the wordmark's look and feel to create unity. Small typographic details, such as right-aligning the *I am…* headlines on the periods, give the site, designed by FORGE, LLC, added sophistication.

GROUPON

San Francisco

More cities ▼

Drawer

Never Miss a Groupon:

email   facebook   rss   twitter

FAQ   How Groupon Works   Get Featured   Recent Deals   facebook connect   Sign in   Join up

Share this deal: facebook   email   twitter

Today's Deal: $100 for 2 1-Hour Massages and Health Consultation. (Value $200)

Time left to buy:

**23 Hours
57 Minutes
13 Seconds**

◄ **Image gallery** ►

0 Tipped! **257**

When 50 groupons are purchased by midnight CDT we all get it!

Qty: 1 @ **$100 Buy**

Let's Do This!

"Some really rad stuff on this page. Keep it going long... 2 mins ago

See all 257 comments | See all 257 groupies

Side Deal

Ad Space

Worth:	**$200**
You Pay:	**$100**
You Save:	**$100 (50%)**

The Low Down

Expires in 1 year. 1 per person, may buy more as gifts. Use in separate visits or split with a friend. First time customers only. Email drweisz@drweisz.com or call 773.598.5851 to schedule appointment.

The Deal-tails

Company Name
1234 Street Avenue
City, ST 00000 Map
www.website.com

Advertise with Groupon

Firebelly's early wireframes for Groupon zoned content into discreet areas, and also included a 960-pixel columnar grid to create a horizontal rhythm. Even at this early stage, information becomes delineated with a range of typographic sizes and weights.

With the wireframe in place and the header content established, Firebelly investigated typographic opportunities for the header content.

Firebelly's final design brought together the structural elements from the initial wireframe with rounded corners on some elements and a dashed outline around the featured deal. Typographic information gets differentiated through a range of sizes, styles, and colors.

Chapter

5 COLOR
PAT

OR +

TERN

"Color is not a physical quality, but a sensation produced in the brain."
—KEN HIEBERT

Seeing and Making Color

COLOR PERCEPTION ▪ Color is a complex element in visual communication, and many variables affect how we experience it. At one time, users were limited to displays that rendered 256 colors, a fraction of the millions we're used to seeing on personal computers and televisions today. Display surfaces can also impact color saturation, or the lack thereof. Some users prefer devices with glossy screens, noting that blacks appear richer because of those shiny surfaces. Others prefer anti-glare (also called matte) screens that prevent light glares, but the downside is that those devices may not deliver fully saturated colors. Or worse yet, they may cast a yellow-brown hue across the display. Environmental conditions will affect how users see not only color, but also the entire content area: too much natural or artificial sunlight, glare from nearby reflective surfaces, and even surrounding colors on furniture, clothing, or walls.

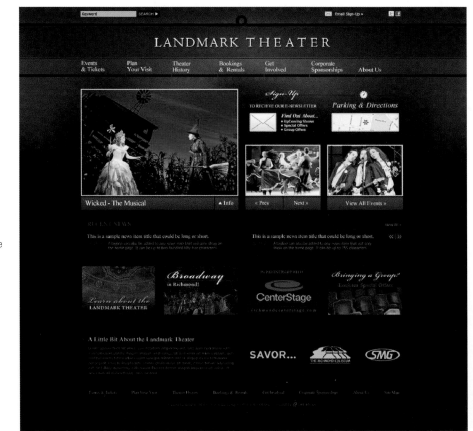

Silverpoint applied color-coded tabs to the Marin School website to help users associate different content areas with a color. This serves to both differentiate the menu items visually, and instill recall from a usability standpoint.

The Landmark Theater interface has colorful event photography that leaps to the foreground, thanks in part to the darker background that carbonhouse applied to the site.

Although the Camp Firebelly website uses an illustrative diorama as a feature image, it uses naturalistic colors where the fire, trees, grassy hills, and clouds mimic real-world colors.

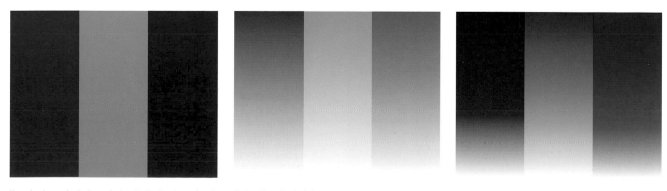

Hue. A color or shade dependent on its dominant wavelength. Red, green, and blue are the dominant digital wavelengths. Each can be mixed to create new hues.

Saturation. A color's intensity, expressed as bright or dull, usually as a distinction from white.

Value. How light or dark a color is.

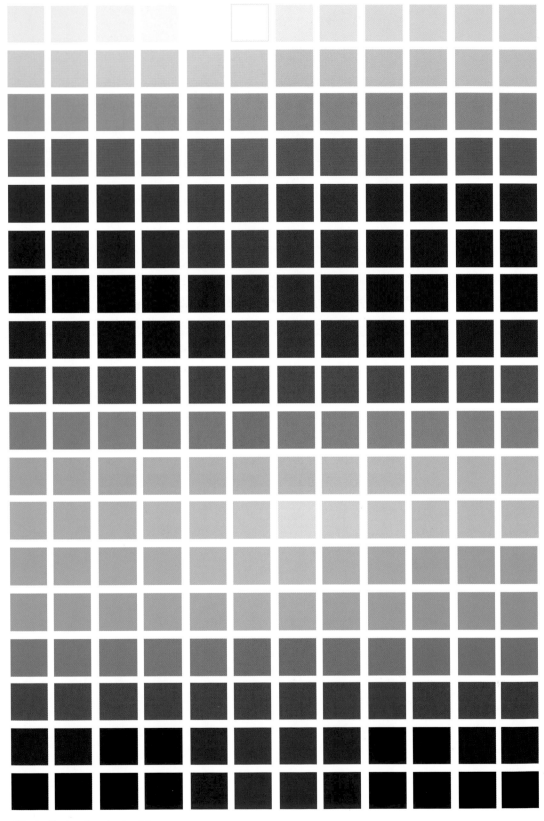

216 color chips from the web-safe palette.

Sixteen Web-Safe Colors

Color	HEX	Red	Green	Blue
White	#FFFFFF	100%	100%	100%
Silver	#C0C0C0	75%	75%	75%
Gray	#808080	50%	50%	50%
Black	#000000	0%	0%	0%
Red	#FF0000	100%	0%	0%
Maroon	#800000	50%	0%	0%
Orange	#FFA500	100%	65%	0%
Yellow	#FFFF00	100%	100%	0%
Olive	#808000	50%	50%	0%
Lime	#00FF00	0%	100%	0%
Green	#008000	0%	50%	0%
Aqua	#00FFFF	0%	100%	100%
Teal	#008080	0%	50%	50%
Blue	#0000FF	0%	0%	100%
Navy	#000080	0%	0%	50%
Fuchsia	#FF00FF	100%	0%	100%
Purple	#800080	50%	0%	50%

Unlike the decimal-based RGB system, the hexadecimal system is a byte-oriented method of building the primary colors of red, green, and blue, along with secondary and tertiary colors. A range of 00 to FF in hexadecimals equates to a range of 0 to 255 in RGB's decimal-based system. The hexadecimal six-digit (or six-character) alphanumeric strings are often used for building colors within HTML and CSS backends. Coding these colors into the backend requires a hash mark (#, also called pound sign or octothorpe) prefix, such as #FFFFFF which equals white or #000000 which equals black. When computers could only display up to 256 colors, the hexadecimal color table helped designers identify colors that would consistently render across devices. But today, many devices use 24-bit rendering of true colors and even most mobile devices have at least 16-bit color

Thanks to richer displays that render millions of colors, carbonhouse's American Airlines Arena site gets a full-color treatment showcasing the breadth of entertainment they offer. Designs such as this were not possible during the days of very limited 256 colors or less.

By overlapping the content surrounding the seating map for the American Airlines Arena website, carbonhouse made those values darker, and in effect, gave the seating map prominence for the viewer.

Each hue in a spectrum has a given wavelength, whether built from the RGB, HSV, or Hex additive color system. But the purity of those colors happens as a result of saturation. Many of us consider a color with more white or less color to be less saturated. Compare the green color emitted from a traffic light with that of a pastel green backlighting used to render a car's speedometer readable at night. The dark green traffic signal and the pastel green backlighting both have the chromatic character of green.

But the pastel green speedometer feels whiter and less green since it has less hue purity, also known as saturation. The words intensity and chroma have also been used to reference the purity of a hue. The green traffic light will have a more intense green, compared to the less intense or neutralized pastel green on the dashboard's speedometer. But even those chromatic qualities can change, depending on surrounding or nearby colors that contrast any given color, known as value and hue contrast.

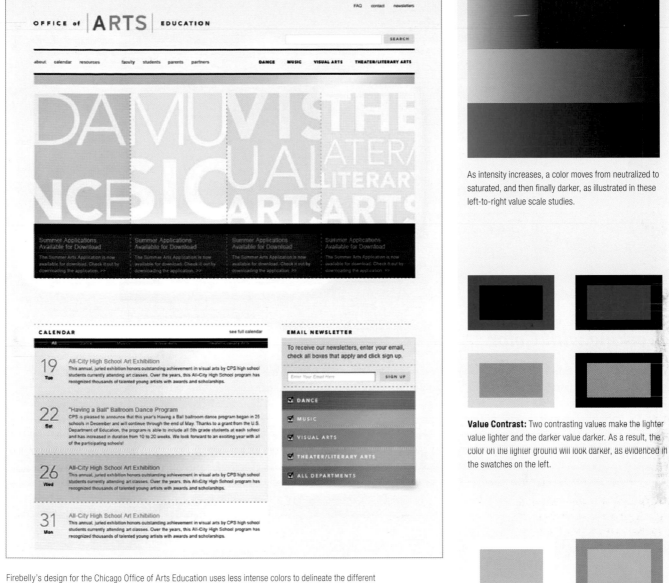

Firebelly's design for the Chicago Office of Arts Education uses less intense colors to delineate the different arts endeavors, but rolling over the menu items creates a more intense value that highlights the selection.

As intensity increases, a color moves from neutralized to saturated, and then finally darker, as illustrated in these left-to-right value scale studies.

Value Contrast: Two contrasting values make the lighter value lighter and the darker value darker. As a result, the color on the lighter ground will look darker, as evidenced in the swatches on the left.

Hue Contrast: Two contrasting hues make the warm color appear warmer and the cool color cooler, but with the neutral gray, notice how the gray in yellow appears somewhat blue.

The College Preparatory School site by Silverpoint has a tiled wood element so that wood fills the background no matter how you size the browser window.

Silverpoint created a realistically marked-up notebook by repeating a single metal ring along the left side of the white frame. A textured pink swatch comes together on the top and bottom of the Why Give? call to action to deliver a painterly effect.

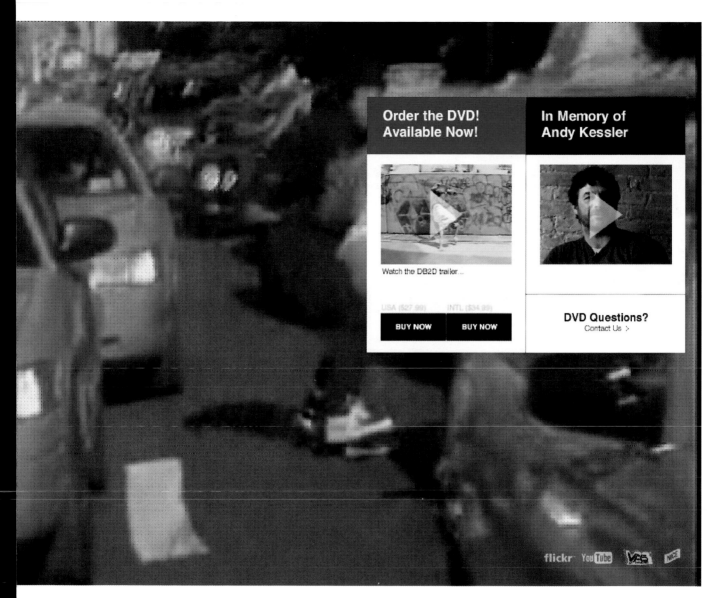

Social Design House layered a dot pattern on top of the background video for the Deathbowl to Downtown site, giving the background the feeling of a coarse television screen.

Visual Properties

These tactile properties give designs naturalistic properties found in natural or artificial materials: wood, sand, stone, metal, water, fire, or canvas. Since digital media uses light to render color, the visual textures that result from coupling dots, lines, or polygons are solely visual, and not tactile. On the other hand, white paint or thread will contain shiny particles in order to reflect light, and wood can be stained with a dull or glossy varnish. But texture is meaningless when devoid of context. Putting a synthetic gray road through the desert seems both absurd and unnecessary.

But when you realize that desert is between Nevada and California in the United States, and the road paved is known as Route 66, the elements carry meaning. Those denotative meanings have a direct meaning for the viewer and elicit images of fast cars, rolling hills, and good days of yesteryear. The final element in that equation pushes those textures into a connotative direction, where nostalgia takes over to give people intimate memories that may be both personal and meaningful.

Chapter

6 IMA
ILLUST

GE +
RATION

"Seeing is not a passive activity. Many different centers of the brain are involved in the relationship of percept and image."

-NATALIA ILYIN

Image Modality

We see and experience things in our daily surroundings that are tangible, physical objects. Many systems exist for capturing those images, one of which most of us carry in our pocket everywhere we go: the camera. Most mobile phones contain a low- to high-quality digital camera, through which we see and capture our daily experiences. When clicked and saved, those images are nothing more than representations: pixels recorded to bytes that render a color or black and white, static, or animated image. Designers and illustrators can also use point, line, plane, texture, and color to compose digital images, be they photorealistic or illustrative.

Big Spaceship utilized sophisticated three-dimensional illustrations to promote the Transformers online game.

It's been said that designers call upon stylistic pasts such as the Bauhaus or Swiss Moderns when capturing or creating images, but thinking about visual qualities instead of stylistic movements provides something more tangible for the designer and client. These qualities may be organic, geometric, handmade, digitally rendered, static, or animated, among others. No matter the adjectives or attributes, it's important to reference imagery and illustration using a system to ground the visuals in a language that the involved parties can understand.

Graphic File Formats

Three formats exist for still images at the time of this writing. Each of them offers advantages and disadvantages when used on the web.

GIF stands for Graphics Interchange Format and uses eight bits of color to create images with up to 256 colors. Use the GIF format for simple graphics such as renderings with one, two, or three colors. Despite the low color output, GIFs offer the opportunity to create transparency: An object's background can be removed in order to let the background color, pattern, photograph, or text show through. Animated GIFs give designers the ability to create simple moving images, where multiple frames give the appearance of movement or color transformation.

JPEG stands for Joint Photographic Experts Group, and because it was developed to handle photographs, it uses twenty-four bits of color to render millions of colors. JPEG files do not offer transparency or animation the way that GIF files do. Many JPEG formatting tools output using lossy methods where compression reduces file size. High compression will reduce the image quality, but will deliver a smaller file size. Low compression will maintain a high level of image quality, but will deliver a larger file size.

PNG, or Portable Network Graphics, has millions of colors like a JPEG with the added bonus of transparency like a GIF. PNG files do not deliver animation the way an animated GIF can. Like GIF and JPEG formats, you can compress a PNG file to make it smaller.

Archrival rendered all of the images on the Ink the Colt 45 site using an illustrative style akin to comic book or cartoon drawings. This gives the interface a light-hearted experience and reinforces the need to ink the can yourself.

Voice used a range of images, some photographic and others symbolic, to represent the different products sold by Rio Coffee.

The photographic form is analogous to what we see with our own eyes in the physical world; however, it has been translated into a flat, two-dimensional form. A website featured in this book is not an actual website, but rather a printed representation of the digital site you'd see on a screen. Digital cameras capture images that can be translated into pixels for us to view on-screen, share via email, or print onto paper or in a book. But even before the capture, saving, and translation, an image must be composed within the viewfinder.

Many of the compositional strategies featured in chapter 3 hold true: symmetry, balance, and white space. Once captured, the image may be saved in its pure and untouched state or transformed through a number of processes. The transformation process can exist in the camera, whereby it gets colorized, neutralized, texturized, blurred, inverted, or rasterized. Such camera-based transformations have grown at an astronomical pace thanks to the plethora of developers looking to bring Photoshop-like filters directly to the camera. Ultimately, the designer should take control of the image in order to improve its quality and composition. Poorly taken photographs can be altered and edited using any number of digital tools, and while it's rare, post-production can turn a lousy image into something useful.

A photographic image, and its exploded 2-in² area details the pixels used.

If each of these illustrated screens displayed at 72 dpi, a 72 dpi image would remain the same size when viewed on the larger display. Some systems allow you to zoom in and fill the screen, but doing so will allow users to see more pixels.

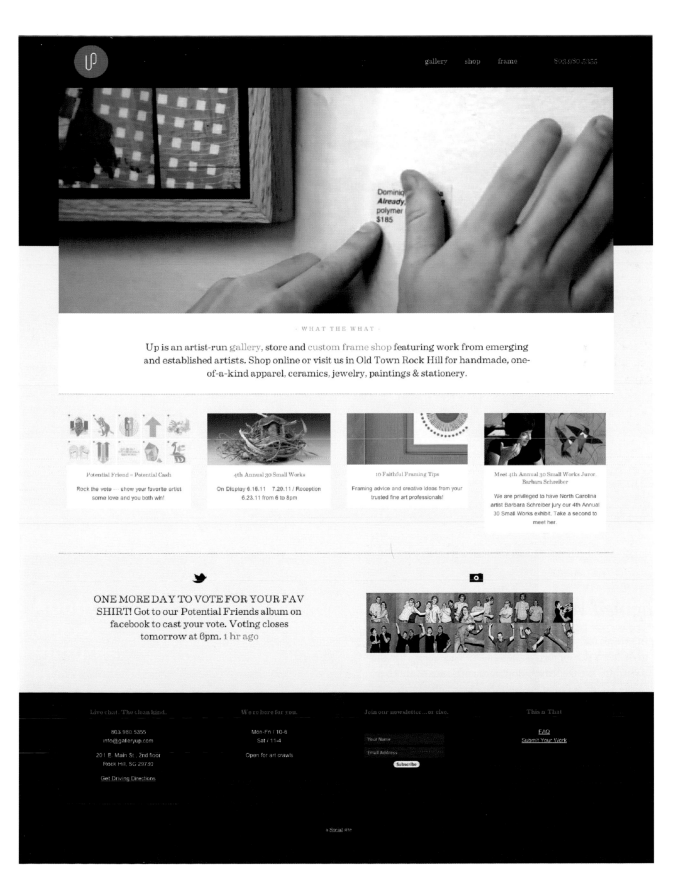

· WHAT THE WHAT ·

Up is an artist-run gallery, store and custom frame shop featuring work from emerging and established artists. Shop online or visit us in Old Town Rock Hill for handmade, one-of-a-kind apparel, ceramics, jewelry, paintings & stationery.

Potential Friend = Potential Cash

Rock the vote — show your favorite artist some love and you both win!

4th Annual 30 Small Works

On Display 6.16.11 – 7.20.11 / Reception 6.23.11 from 6 to 8pm

10 Faithful Framing Tips

Framing advice and creative ideas from your trusted fine art professionals!

Meet 4th Annual 30 Small Works Juror, Barbara Schreiber

We are privileged to have North Carolina artist Barbara Schreiber jury our 4th Annual 30 Small Works exhibit. Take a second to meet her.

ONE MORE DAY TO VOTE FOR YOUR FAV SHIRT! Got to our Potential Friends album on facebook to cast your vote. Voting closes tomorrow at 6pm. 1 hr ago

Live chat. The clean kind.

803.980.5355
info@galleryup.com

201 E. Main St., 2nd floor
Rock Hill, SC 29730

Get Driving Directions

We're here for you.

Mon-Fri / 10-6
Sat / 11-4

Open for art crawls

Join our newsletter...or else.

Your Name
Email Address

Subscribe

This n That

FAQ
Submit Your Work

a Norial site

Social Design House's close-up photography on the Gallery Up website delivers a look at the fine detail that goes into preparing an exhibition.

Using cultural signifiers and symbols can speak directly to an audience, fostering a trustworthy relationship. Like color, images carry cultural significance. Some images can change meaning depending on the cultural lens you're looking through. Others are universal.

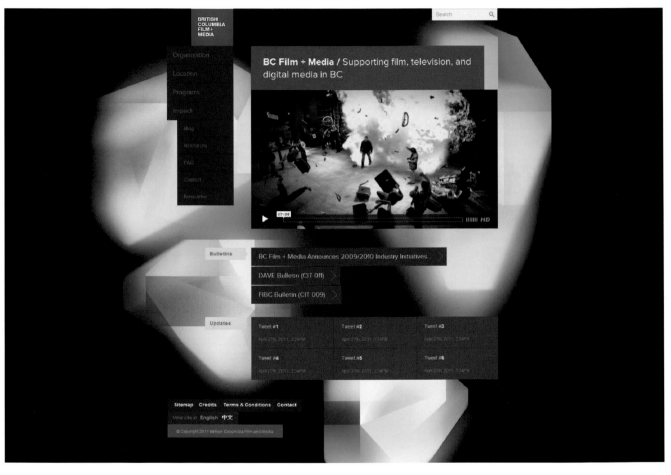

When smashLAB designed the British Columbia Film + Media website, they were aware of how quickly media changes. The resultant design uses responsive menus, colorful imagery, and an ambient background that speaks to cutting-edge media.

Gopal Raju is a designer, developer, and blogger from India. When searching for a domain name for his portfolio, he went with the prefix Indo- that is often used to indicate India. He illustrated five of the ten incarnations of Lord Vishnu to create a unique concept for his IndoFolio website: Matsya, Kurma, Krishna (also known as Gopal), Varaha, and Vamana.

When version industries (v) designed a site for the Irish comedian Andrew Maxwell, they captured his style and attitude by putting you face to face with articles about him, all read at your local, greasy diner.

Compositionally, Belmer Negrillo designed Jairo Goldflus's website so that photographs appear large, maintaining their proportion no matter the browser size. Chromatically, the site's background is neither black, nor white, nor gray, but rather changes to complement the featured image.

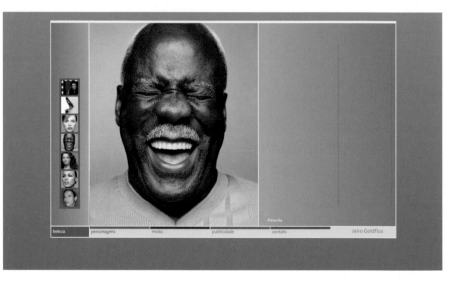

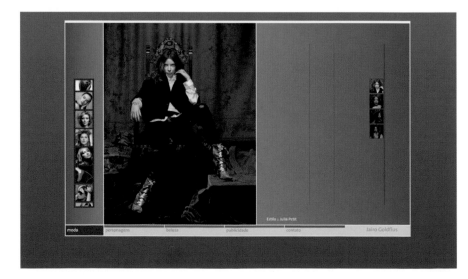

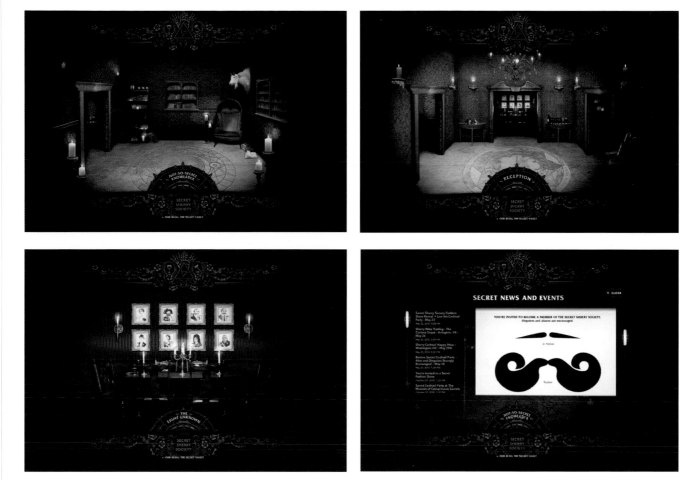

Archrival delivers a first-person experience that takes users through a three-dimensional environment much like a video game. The pleasure comes from moving around the space and going so far as accepting a moustache to disguise your persona.

Augmented reality combines material from our real environment with its digitally rendered equivalent with added visual material. Rishi Sodha of 2Creatives demonstrates how a marker on a sheet of paper cues a computer display to render an animated movie.

Chapter

7 THE

ONLINE BRAND

"The good and bad of the digital realm is that it's transitory and dynamic. So a consumer's expectation for a brand is the same."
—TAN LE

Brand Basics

The word "brand" has become so mainstream that you can go to the shopping mall and hear customers talking about how the Nike brand differs from Adidas. But a brand is more than just a shoe you see in a sales display. It amounts to everything that goes into a product, and manifests itself with cooperation among the stakeholders, employees, patrons, and consumers. It can be a top-down hierarchy where the stakeholders strive to make an entity succeed and create an atmosphere and environment that motivates the employees to do the same by delivering promises, products, values, and services to the general public. Or it can happen from the outside in, where the users cultivate content using a given framework, as in the case of Facebook.

Ideally, a brand expert will assist the institution in strategizing the approach, whether needed for a new company, new product launch, name change, revitalization, integration, or merger. The term "touchpoint" has been used to describe the methods for extending the brand given any of the aforementioned objectives. Touchpoints can strengthen a brand and communicate its value or values. They are essential to a brand's success, and will resonate physically or mentally with people. Consider the word itself: touch. You can physically touch something and feel its surface, but you can also be touched by something on an emotional level.

When you consider David Berlo's communication process, there are numerous channels for sending a message and, in turn, for extending a brand. A message can be encoded in such a way that only those who are privy to the code will understand it. It can use language, art, gesture, or physical structures. Brands can promote their products using smell, like the aroma you intake when passing by a McDonald's, which leads you to crave French fries. Tasting, touching, hearing, and seeing can all become touchpoints.

And with digital media enabling three of those channels (many devices have touch interaction), it has become a powerful means for extending a brand. Digital media allows for brands to reach out through email, websites, blogs, gaming, social media, audio, and video. Each category has its own set of tertiary deliverables. An email can be informational, teaching people about how a new product will improve their day-to-day production. An email can also contain a coupon, pushing for a sale with the promise of a discount. Blogs can build a community where patrons who are loyal to the brand come to share their good experiences, as well as bad ones. And because digital communication happens at any time through the use of handheld devices such as mobile phones, companies have to take the good and the bad.

Consumers become critics, who tout ways to improve products. They've even been known to create Facebook pages to complain about a new brand identity, as so many people did when The Gap launched their new mark in 2010. In the end The Gap yielded and reverted back to the original logo. The customer was right, and the customer won thanks to digital media. Tan Le, former creative director at Landor and Young & Rubicam Brands, and current VP and design director at Miller Zell, makes this suggestion: "A brand's essence is owned by the company that makes the brand, and expressed to consumers through its form and communications. That's what makes it unique, genuine, and differentiated. Much of that is lost if that control becomes dictated by consumers instead of the company."

IDENTITIES ▪ Oftentimes we confuse the brand identity with the brand itself. A brand is the meta-element, whereas the brand identity is the micro-element. The brand identity is a verbal and/or visual component used to build the brand platform. The identity will resonate with all of the involved parties, and be memorable enough to distinguish it from the competition and surrounding noise. Symbols such as logos, emblems, and wordmarks are used to distill a brand into a graphic element. Email newsletters, websites, Twitter streams, Facebook pages, mobile apps, and even YouTube videos comprise some of the digital communications that reach patrons, customers, and citizens on a daily basis—or even more frequently. Above all, the brand identity will be appropriate for the brand, and assist with building awareness to stimulate use, belief, consumption, and purchase. It engages the viewer through sensorial means with supporting visual elements striving to elicit trust and reliability. How can something so simple do so many things? Ultimately, it's not the mark itself that does this, but the association people make with the mark. The mark points to the bigger picture—the brand—to connect with viewers on more than just a visual level. The next time you notice the Nike swoosh, consider all of the things that rush through your mind.

Wordmarks are built from an acronym or name. When creating their own identity, Social Design House simplified their name down to Social with this flowing script.

Pictorials use a recognizable, illustrative, or stylized image. Joshua Mauldin created the Azrotech identity by pairing Azro the robot's simplified head with the Azrotech wordmark. Azro's expression changes depending on what part of the site you visit.

Lettermarks are shorter, and use one or more glyphs to enable quick identification and recall. UnderConsideration shortened their blog For Print Only into simply FPO, a commonly used term among designers and printers.

Abstractions can look representational or nonrepresentational, and carry indirect, literal, or metaphorical meaning. The SlideRoom wordmark is set in a traditional and established serif face, Garamond, to elicit a time-tested quality. The abstraction to the left, designed by A.J. Fitzpatrick in collaboration with the SlideRoom team, has no literal reference, but the sinewy shape was found in letterforms, light emissions, and Venn diagrams that inspired it.

Icons, such as those found on a computer's graphic interface, can use text and image to represent a file, many files, software, hardware, processes, or communication. Acqualia's Soulver icon visualizes the functions of its calculator app in one singular image in an almost narrative fashion.

Emblems connect pictorial elements with wordmarks or letterforms. Undrln was created to serve as a venue for critical discussion on advertising initiatives. Their emblem unifies typography, iconography, and geometric shapes into a singular mark.

Look and Feel

The term look and feel has been associated with digital design since the advent of HTML and the Internet. It had become synonymous with the outer skin wrapped around the backend. Composition, layout, color, imagery, typography, sequence, motion graphics, animation, and sound all factor into the look and feel. Traditional designers will recognize many of those elements, as they're key in designing for print media. Motion graphics, animation, and sound are not always key to a digital experience, especially since platforms and plug-ins don't always coexist together, as exemplified by Apple taking a pass on Flash plug-ins operating on Safari's mobile iOS browser.

Even information architecture can aid in the brand identity. Corporate entities that appear together will deliver a solid, unified front for the stakeholders, employees, and consumers. Corporate entities that operate better across brand channels and through differing demographics may not want to do such a thing. For years, the Swedish car manufacturer Saab was an affiliate of General Motors, but few Saab customers realized that. Keeping the brands segmented ensured that Saab maintained its identity without appearing to be under the umbrella of General Motors. Content, sound, imagery, motion graphics, color, typography, and social exchanges can all become part of the online look and feel built into the brand identity.

Name:

What is the existing name?

What are the competitors' names?

What legal criteria will factor into the name?

Does the name need to be cross-cultural?

How does the name work in the context of the brand image, products, and placement?

Is the name searchable on the Internet?

Is the name easy to recall?

Will the name get confused with another brand?

Design:

Is the layout logical and appropriate?

Is it simple enough for people to interact with?

Can they get help quickly and easily?

Is the design creative just to be creative, or does it have purpose?

Has careful exploration been conducted, or did you settle on something too quickly?

Does the design hold up well across different media sizes and resolutions?

Does the information architecture meet the users' needs or the institutions'?

Have resources balanced technology and design to deliver a pleasurable experience?

Typography:

Can the typeface convey a personality?

Will the typography function at various sizes?

Does the typography look different enough from the competitor?

What about cultural connotations?

Is there a budget to design a unique typeface just for the brand?

Rich Media:

Can rich media extend the brand and communicate a message?

Is there a budget for sound, motion graphics, and/or video?

Can it be done in-house?

Can people create their own rich media and share it through a community?

If the budget is limited, is there one rich media channel that must be employed?

Can sound and imagery enrich the brand?

How can sound be used with navigational cues or menus?

Color:

Will the color resonate with viewers?

Is it similar to competitors' color identities?

How does the color function when paired with other colors?

What happens when items are overlaid on white, gray, or black?

Can color relate to the brand architecture, products, or heritage?

What happens if the saturation is changed?

Should there be a print palette and a separate digital palette?

Can the color get its own name?

Imagery:

Will the images be representational or non-representational?

Will they be photographic or illustrative?

Will color get used abundantly or sparingly?

How will the imagery translate from one media to the next, be it small or large?

What connotation or denotation will the imagery deliver?

Will the images be proprietary and copyrighted or open for the general public to use, change, and share?

Tan Le, former creative director at Landor and Young & Rubicam Brands, is the current VP and design director at Miller Zell.

The key measurement of a brand's effectiveness is media-agnostic, because most brands must transcend channels and communicate to multiple consumer touchpoints. So the strategic platform of a brand—its attributes, promise, value, and so on—should be the same regardless of whether the brand is foil embossed on a product package, or doing an animated cartwheel on a website. If a brand is expressed on a package, consumers would expect a tactile, multisurface engagement—sequential sides, flip-open panels, dimensional surfaces, and similar elements. If a brand is expressed in a retail space, then consumers would expect scale, a more immersive experience, and so on. So the same difference in expectation is true of digital brands.

The good and bad of the digital realm is that it's transitory and dynamic. So consumers' expectations for a brand are the same. A digital brand shouldn't cause an epileptic seizure, but it should take advantage of the availability of motion, sequential storytelling, and seamless scale transitions.

Getting consumer insights is almost always a helpful thing for brand development. But insights are just guidance, and should never be mistaken for commands. In other words, a brand should never be art-directed by a consumer group—regardless of whether it's a focus group, blog mob, crowdsourcing, public opinion poll, or whatever. Of course, the public has every right to voice their opinions through their pocketbooks—which is what The Gap and Tropicana feared would result. So they pulled their rebrands and went back to what was safe. But that's a gutless, lazy way to do branding. In both cases, the failure meant that something went wrong in the research process, not the rebrand itself. The subsequent public backlash and retread is damage control.

Feedback can be a good thing, but only if it's channeled smartly, and used in the correct stage of brand development. Brand research and development should take advantage of these new, growing, and free channels of consumer feedback. Quantitative and qualitative research techniques should be stepped up to reflect a new era in public opinion sourcing. Meeting that challenge would be a good thing for branding. Let the public speak, and listen and respond. But never let them dictate the design.

With mobile digital domains, the rules of brand engagement with customers are expanding and morphing daily. The media is similar to traditional broadcast, but with a shorter attention span. Brands will need to say more, and be much quicker about it. And the amount of information that brands will have to compete with will also exponentially grow. So brands will have to be more unique, memorable, and inventive.

When Studiobanks designed sites for Discovery Place, the Charlotte Nature Museum, and Discovery Place KIDS, they created a unified layout and logo placement to link the brand image. Colors, image styles, and typographic nuances change from one to the next so that each museum speaks a unique language.

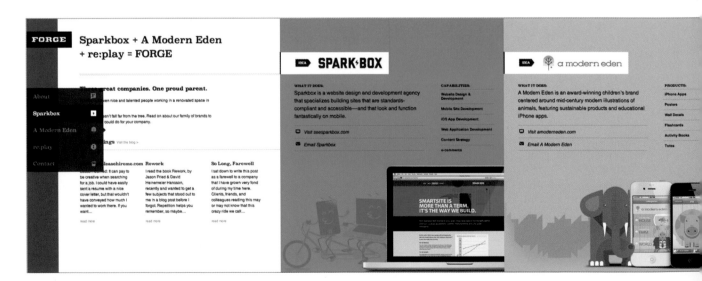

FORGE, LLC, needed to deliver a unified front among its three creative companies: Sparkbox, A Modern Eden, and re:play. This singular layout brings the three companies together and also functions as a road map that guides users from one creative specialist to another.

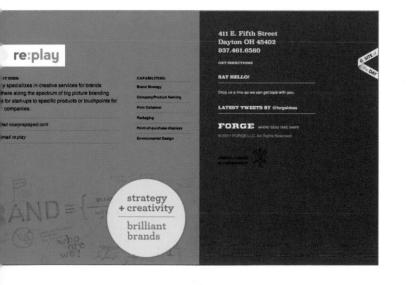

Digital Touchpoints

Hardware

Software

Apps

Add-ons

Games

Digital Services

Learning Tools

Utilities

Videos

Video Conferences or Conventions

Music

Spoken Word

Online Advertising

Marketing

Banners

Twitter Feeds

Facebook Pages

Facebook Profiles

Websites

Blogs

Social Media

Email Newsletters

Email

Electronic Publications

Digital Annual Reports

Audio Books

Online Forms

SlideRoom is an online applicant management system that handles media, forms, and references in one place. An online newsletter tells users about new features, even crediting the users themselves: "You spoke, we listened!" A call to action at the newsletter's closing takes you to the online blog so that you can follow SlideRoom happenings daily. In addition to highlighting new features, the blog even goes as far as educating people about the design process SlideRoom went through to update their site's look and feel.

SlideRoom

AUGUST 2011

New features: You spoke, we listened!

Collect Formatted Documents

Administrators may now request specific formatted documents (resumes, budgets etc.) separate from portfolio media. Applicant instructions are included with each request. **Learn more**

More Media Types and Sizes

SlideRoom has greatly expanded the number of file types accepted (e.g. widely used .mp4 videos). Additionally, should you need to collect print quality images, longer videos or audio files, you may opt-in to receive much larger files. **Learn more**

More Flexibility with References

Administrators may now set the due-date displayed to recommenders. Additionally, applicants may change and resend unfulfilled reference requests if needed, even on completed submissions. **Learn more**

Follow our blog to stay up to date on new features and enhancements.

Go ›

As half agency and half production company, Lucky positions itself at the center of concept, production, and media. The New York-based company writes, produces, and directs viral films and branded content. Lifeislottery created a solid and meaningful online introduction to the Lucky brand, by capturing their unique voice and approach to content.

Engagement

In today's digital age, brands have to deliver an engaging experience. But what are the key considerations brands need to have when it comes to getting themselves into the digital realm? Tan Le suggests brands should be media-neutral: "The key measurements of a brand's effectiveness are media-agnostic, because most brands must transcend channels and communicate to multiple consumer touchpoints. So the strategic platform of a brand—its attributes, promise, value, and so on—should be the same regardless of whether the brand is foil embossed on a product package, or doing an animated cartwheel on a website."

And through the power of online communication and social networking, the citizen/designer can now pass judgment on a brand and become heard. When The Gap released a revised mark in 2010, the public shot it down through blogs, Facebook pages, tweets, and exchanged comments on the aforementioned. The general public can now tell a brand how good or bad it's doing, judging every sense of its performance, including, but not limited to, the digital image it projects. Tan Le feels this can be somewhat helpful: "Brand research and development should take advantage of these new, growing, and free channels of consumer feedback. Quantitative and qualitative research techniques should be stepped up to reflect a new era in public opinion sourcing."

GOOD's website maintains the same framework because its content changes so frequently. When users come to the site, they can browse through the articles without having to learn a new system all over again.

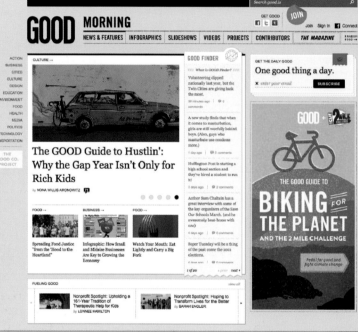

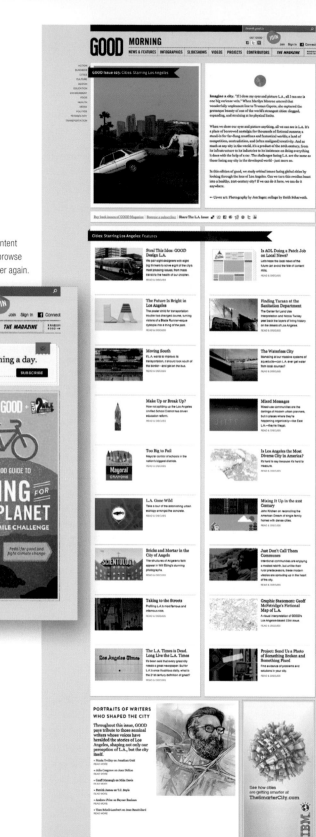

Lifeislottery also had to create the ultimate online branded viral video database for The Viral Collection, an offshoot of the Lucky brand. Presentation of video and overall display of aggregated information needed to be designed in a way that was intuitive, fun, scalable, and fast. A morass of images and information come together and are viewable on multiple devices.

FLEXIBILITY ■ can help a brand morph depending on certain factors. Externally, the brand may have a wide range of demographics that it appeals to. One example would be Nike, which manufactures and distributes sports and active wear for men and women of all ages. Nike's consumers come in all shapes and sizes, just like the Nike products that they use. Some may play basketball, and others baseball. Some live in Europe and others in South America. They are old and they are young. Culturally, the brand needs to speak to each demographic in an authentic and trustworthy way, but the digital manifestation of that visual language can change depending on the products, economy, culture, demographic, and even season. But what if the content itself is the product delivered? News can be considered a product in the same way that shoes, shirts, and socks can, only the news isn't a physical entity that you can order and have delivered to your mailbox.

Readers value news that's timely, relevant, and accessible. GOOD delivers all of that in its printed magazine, and anybody can get that content by visiting Good.is to read and interact with content in a more immediate way. If Nike can change their image depending on the product, consumer, culture, and season, can GOOD do the same online? GOOD has content changing on a regular basis, but their online framework stays the same so that you can get to what you want: the content. While Nike can have a multitude of sites with differing interfaces, products, and look and feel, GOOD gives consumers a reassurance that says "We won't make you work too hard to find what you need." GOOD's creative director, Casey Caplowe, discusses the need for always making improvements: "We do weekly releases and improvements. Some are more noticeable than others, but stuff is always in the works."

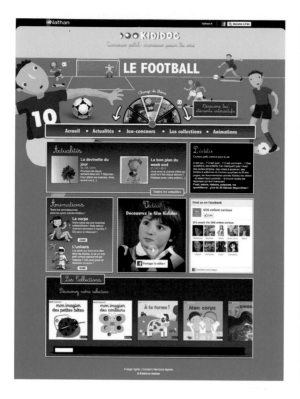

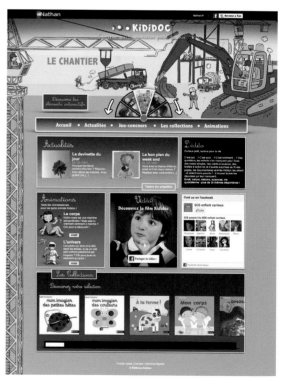

Ultranoir designed the Kididoc website with playfulness in mind, giving users four different interface skins to choose from, including pirates, dinosaurs, soccer, and construction. This added flexibility speaks to the animated nature of Kididoc products, and the range of subjects they provide.

Instrument designed the Nike Sports Research Lab, Nike 6.0 iDNation, and Nike 6.0 Women's Collection with rich interfaces. Each possesses visual qualities unique unto itself, but each one is Nike. Because Nike speaks to a wide and deep demographic, its digital identity can flex and morph depending on the brand's strategic objectives.

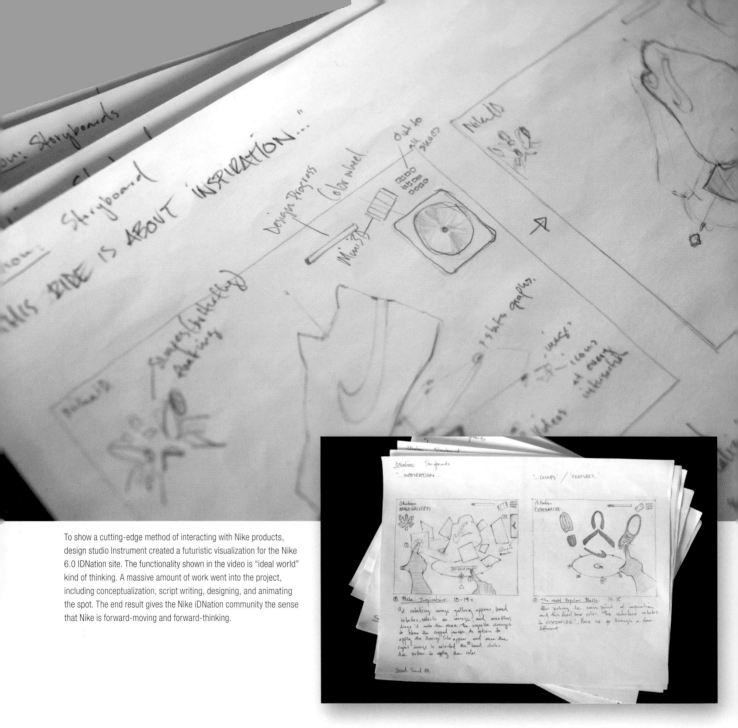

To show a cutting-edge method of interacting with Nike products, design studio Instrument created a futuristic visualization for the Nike 6.0 IDNation site. The functionality shown in the video is "ideal world" kind of thinking. A massive amount of work went into the project, including conceptualization, script writing, designing, and animating the spot. The end result gives the Nike iDNation community the sense that Nike is forward-moving and forward-thinking.

How can you capture the way somebody will interact with a brand, its products, and fellow brand enthusiasts? Attitude and emotion are as good a place as any to start. In speaking and writing terms this is often called voice, but visuals can possess a voice in much the same way that language and speech can. A digital interface synthesizes language, color, tone, texture, imagery, illustration, and composition, but it's the conceptual direction that gives it that voice. Language plays a large role in the voice, but imagery can convey attitude with just as much force, although the imagery must be direct enough to get the point across without any mystery.

GPO Hotel approached Twofold Creative to design and build a site that reflected their reputation as one of Brisbane's premier club venues. The slick online presence has current events with photo galleries capturing those memories. If the site were devoid of any text, a user would be able to see that this was a place to be seen at.

When users click to learn more about the Ultranoir agency, they meet a motley group of characters with unique personalities. Each one touts an Ultranoir area of expertise in a fun way, telling clients and soon-to-be-clients, "We like our job and we have fun doing it."

As part of UnderConsideration's blogosphere, Brand New has become an authoritative website covering all things related to corporate and brand identity work. Some of the most ardent discussions about logos and corporate identity can be found daily at the site.

With Brand New taking on a life of its own, UnderConsideration launched the Brand New conferences—a perfect example of how an online entity successfully morphed from something content-rich, built around a community, and into a full-fledged experience.

When Twofold Creative had to promote the HP House kickoff event, the concept needed to be fresh and colorful, akin to a summer fiesta. The end result marries colorful artwork with in-your-face photography, making it the summer place to be.

The saying "Content is King" is just as important today as it was in the twentieth century. A website may have bells and whistles galore, but if there's nothing substantial beneath that veneer, nobody will want to take the time to remain there and engage with it. Creating community, dialog, and education are just some of the ways a brand can extend itself to the masses. When users recognize a brand as valuable because it's exclusive, they may have more interest in visiting. In the early 2000s, Google began its now-infamous Gmail service, but not everyone could get an address. Addresses were handed out in limited supply, and each Gmail user could "invite" his friends or family to get an address as well. Facebook operated in a similar way when it expanded to college campuses one by one, available only to those with an .edu web address.

Today, each of those tools has become so popular as to be called conventional. In a similar way, the TED talks were invite-only, but when the brand launched its website, the masses could partake in watching the inspirational and creative lectures in front of their own personal computer. This gives people a sense of community that is similar to the events themselves: You're not at TED, but you can watch the lectures as they happened. Digital environments that act as information repositories and news forums, and that have rich and valuable content with the value-add of a community, pay out in dividends. The success of blogs, Facebook, and Twitter only reinforces this position. And many of the sites that were successful in the early 2000s continue to be successful today because they recognized that content and community matter.

TED Ideas worth spreading

Themes	Joining TED	Sign Out	About TED
Talks	Member Profiles	My Account	TEDConferences
Speakers	Member Videos	My Profile	TEDBlog
			TEDPrize

Explore 105 TED talks from remarkable people

Search ▶

Focus on:

- ■ All
- □ Technology
- □ Entertainment
- □ Design
- □ Business
- □ Science
- □ Arts
- □ Global
- □ Staff picks

Resize by:

- ■ Most talks
- □ Newest updates
- □ Most emailed
- □ Most discussed
- □ Most activity

View as list »

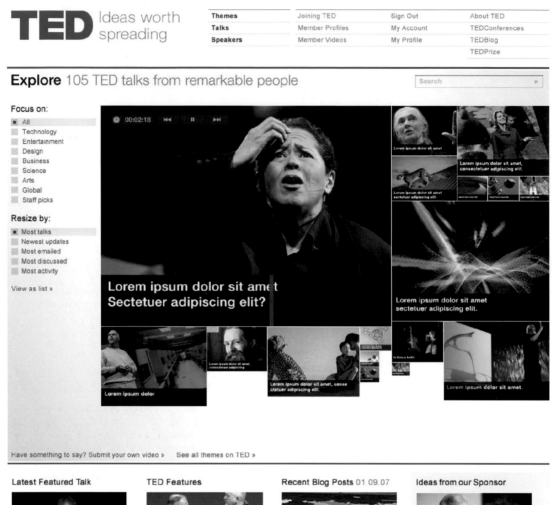

00:02:18

Lorem ipsum dolor sit amet

Lorem ipsum dolor sit amet, consectetuer adipiscing elit.

Lorem ipsum dolor sit amet Sectetuer adipiscing elit?

Lorem ipsum dolor sit amet sectetuer adipiscing elit.

Lorem ipsum dolor

Lorem ipsum dolor sit amet, consectetuer adipiscing

Lorem ipsum dolor sit amet, consectetuer adipiscing elit.

Lorem ipsum dolor sit amet.

Have something to say? Submit your own video »   See all themes on TED »

Latest Featured Talk	**TED Features**	**Recent Blog Posts** 01.09.07	**Ideas from our Sponsor**

Michael Shermer	**'07 TEDprize Winners Announced**	Choreography of a JetBlue terminal	**BMW CEO Helmut Panke:**
Why People Believe Weird Things	Nulla facilisi. Etiam turpis magnaza,	DNA is the new fossil record	*Hydrogen is the future of fuel*
Venenatis non, consecter atnala,	venenatis non, consecter atnala,	A Working Hundred Dollar Laptop	venenatis non, consecter akatnala,
fermentum in, erat. More »	fermentum in erat. More »	Ads we love: Honda "Choir"	fermentum erat. Oy suspen more »

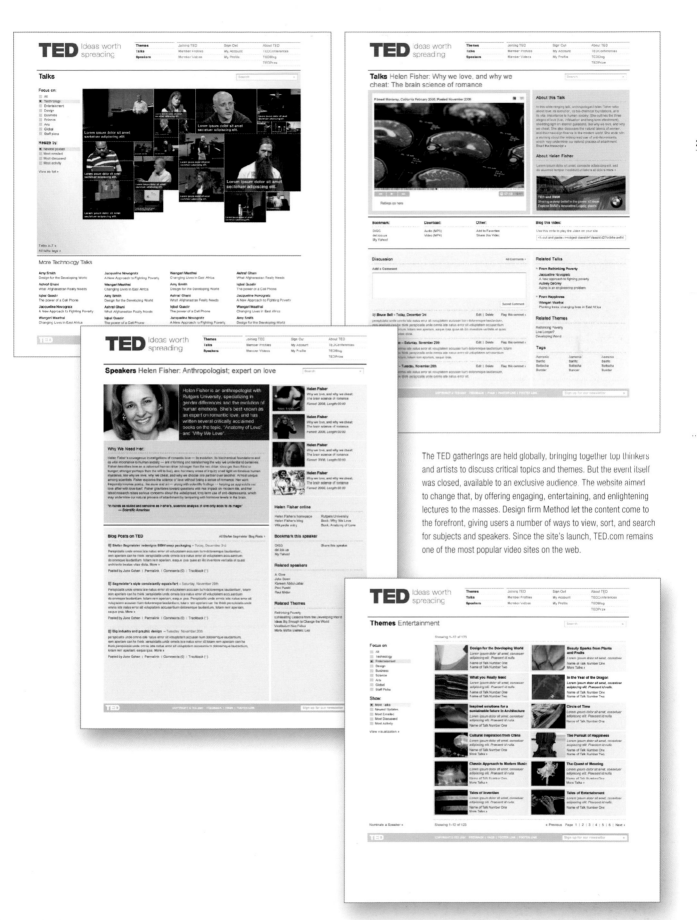

The TED gatherings are held globally, bringing together top thinkers and artists to discuss critical topics and themes. But the event itself was closed, available to an exclusive audience. The website aimed to change that, by offering engaging, entertaining, and enlightening lectures to the masses. Design firm Method let the content come to the forefront, giving users a number of ways to view, sort, and search for subjects and speakers. Since the site's launch, TED.com remains one of the most popular video sites on the web.

Adaptable Design (also Elastic Design): A flexible design in which composition, typography, and images change to match large or small screens.

Alpha Channel Transparency: A variable built into PNG images that allows you to see through an image to an element behind it.

Animation: A sequence of images that give the illusion of motion or movement.

Anti-Aliasing: The process of blurring a line or changing its pixels to give the line a smoother appearance.

Application (App): Computer software designed to perform a specific task, a set of tasks, or multiple operations. Can include, but is not limited to, photo editing, word processing, email communication and management, and media recording/playing/editing.

Aspect Ratio: The width to height relationship of a digital display. Pan and scan televisions from the twentieth century had a 4:3 aspect ratio, where 4 is the width and 3 is the height. Today's film and DVD media have a 1.85:1 aspect ratio, and many digital displays have widescreen aspect ratios of 16:9 or 16:10.

Augmented Reality (AR): Seeing and experiencing real-world images on a digital screen with additional objects or information inserted in the digital display. Requires a digital display and a digital camera.

Backend (or Back End, also called Programming or Development): The code, instructions, controls, and/or operations that happen behind the frontend; often invisible to the end-user, who interfaces with the media. Programmers specialize in this area of production; however, graphic or interface designers have also been known to do this work.

Bandwidth: The capacity of digital or analog transmissions across a network. Smaller bandwidths will run slower by delivering less content in a given time period, and wider (or fatter) bandwidths will run faster by delivering more content during said time period.

Bitmap: Images, fonts, or moving images composed of pixels. Differs from vector, scalable vector graphic, paths, and outlines.

Blog: A type of website or part of a website that includes frequently updated content along with comments from readers. Many blog entries often list material in reverse-chronological order, with the most recent posts featured at the top of the site.

Body Text: Also referred to as body copy, body type, or text type, the paragraphs in a document that comprise the bulk of its content. Body text should be composed in a legible and readable style and size. The size preference can change from user to user and from device to device, but is generally set in 14 pixels or larger. Mobile devices may require smaller text, desktops and televisions may require larger text.

Brand: The complete package a company, institution, or individual delivers to identify itself. Visually, a brand can include the name, logo, and emblem, but it is much larger than a mere graphic identity. People, perception, promise, product, purpose, position, plan, and philosophy are some of the issues and influences that go into brand building.

Browser: A software tool used for finding and displaying resources found on the Internet or an intranet. Chrome, Explorer, Opera, Firefox, and Safari are examples used on computer systems.

Clipboard: The area in RAM memory that holds what you last cut or copied. Pasting from the clipboard inserts the contents into the document.

Crash: The failure of commands, whether initiated by you, an input device, or the computer.

CSS (Cascading Style Sheet): A semantic write-up that describes look and formatting, commonly used for web pages such as those marked up in HTML and XHTML. Also employed with other backends such as XML, SVG, and SWF.

Cursor: A symbol on a digital display that acts as a pointer. It may be a graphic representation such as an arrow or hand, but your finger can also act as a cursor used for touching, clicking, selecting, and moving content.

Data Scraping: A slang term that refers to referencing, importing, or linking to content that exists outside of a digital framework, such as a site that loads database content from a remote URL.

Developer (also called Programmer): A person who creates the backend that makes a frontend design function or animate for the user.

Display Text: Larger, bolder, or more noticeable text used for headlines or other attention-getting purposes. Oftentimes, displays text functions to pull the reader in to read the body text.

Div: Similar to a grid unit, this generic element appears marked up in HTML and CSS and can contain text, imagery, animations, form fields, or buttons.

Dots Per Inch (DPI): A physical measurement for printing density, specifically the number of individual printed dots that can be placed in a line within the span of 1 inch (2.5 cm). Different devices print at different dpi and in many cases 300 dpi or higher will give the best quality. The dpi may correlate with image resolution such as pixels per inch (ppi).

Dumb Quotes: The term used to describe prime marks when set incorrectly as quotation marks or apostrophes.

Early Adopter: A person who acquires new technology before it has reached the consumer market, or as soon as it arrives. Early adopters are often ahead of the curve, and willing to cope with unforeseeable challenges that the new technology will bring.

Em: A unit of measurement equal to the square of a font's point size. It was traditionally the width of a font's widest letter, oftentimes the uppercase *M*.

Em Dash: A dash equal to the width of one em.

En: A unit of measurement that equals one-half the width of one em.

En Dash: A dash measuring one en wide, oftentimes indicating a range of values.

End-User: The audience that a design is intended for.

Experience Designer: In the late 1990s and early 2000s, graphic designers, interactive designers, environmental designers, and packaging designers, among others, began referring to themselves in this manner to highlight how users interact with their designs. This term continues to be used in general terms, and goes beyond media and tools.

Font: The physical or digital embodiment of a glyph set that is used for typesetting, often used interchangeably with the word typeface.

Font Referencing (also called Font Substitution): Using an online service such as Typekit to render a website's text in a font that does not reside on the end-user's system.

Frontend (or Front End, also called Interface Design, User Interface Design): The text, colors, buttons, imagery, animation, movies, menus, and/or interactivity a user interfaces with when viewing electronic media on her computer, tablet, or handheld. Designers will create the frontend using a range of software; however, graphic designers have been known to design these interfaces without doing any of the backend whatsoever.

GIF (Graphics Interchange Format): A file format that uses eight bits of color to create digital images with up to 256 colors. Use the GIF format for simple graphics such as renderings with one, two, or three colors. Despite the low color output, GIFs offer the opportunity to create transparency: An object's background can be removed in order to let the background color, pattern, photograph, or text show through. Animated GIFs give designers the ability to create simple moving images, where multiple frames give the appearance of movement or color transformation.

Gradient: A visual transition whereby a color gradually or immediately transforms from one hue, value, or saturation into another.

Grid: A layout tool that is composed of horizontal lines intersecting with vertical lines, creating a system of columns, modules, and intervals for composing visual media with unity and variety.

GUI (Graphical User Interface, pronounced GOO-ee): A series of visual devices that come together on a computer's visual display to deliver digital content. An umbrella term that includes WUI underneath it.

Heuristics (also called Heuristic Evaluation, after Molich and Nielsen): The science behind user testing that evaluates a design's successes and failures. This diverse practice uses a number of metrics to assess electronic media such as websites, computer software, or digital kiosks.

Hexadecimal Colors: A byte-oriented method of building the primary colors of red, green, and blue, along with secondary and tertiary colors. A range of 00 to FF in hexadecimals equates to a range of 0 to 255 in RGB's decimal-based system. The hexadecimal six-digit (or six-character) alphanumeric strings are often used for building colors within HTML and CSS backends. Adding these colors into the backend requires a hash mark (#) prefix, such as #FFFFFF which equals white or #000000 which equals black.

HTML (HyperText Markup Language): The preferred markup for crafting web pages. It uses elements to construct compositions and layouts, and can have additional attributes and functions using CSS and JavaScript.

HTTP (Hypertext Transfer Protocol): A method used to transfer HTML documents from one computer to another via the Internet.

Icon: A graphic representation, such as an image of a file, folder, disk, or application. Can also communicate an activity or process.

Inbetweening (also called Tweening): Creating intermediate frames between two similar or different images to give the appearance of change, transition, movement, coloration, or discoloration. Inbetweening has been used in traditional cel-based animation as well as computer animation, and is a mainstay in Adobe's Flash software.

Information Architecture: Composing content or a concept using a systematic method. Oftentimes the method is visual, but it can be purely text-based as well, as in the case of outlines. Often attributed to Richard Saul Wurman.

Input: Any method used to deliver information to a digital device. Common examples include keyboards, mice, and touchscreens. May include video cameras and microphones.

Interaction: The way media affects people through behavior, pathways, destinations, solutions, or requests. A two-way exchange happens where input and output deliver results for the user, and can result in communication, feedback, or entertainment, among other deliverables.

Interactive Designer: Generally speaking, all designers are interactive designers since users work with and interface with the objects they make. However, an interactive designer focuses on not only the user interface, but also the human–computer interaction, and may have a strong background in heuristics or psychology and cognitive science.

Interface: A visual device such as a metaphor that enables people to interact with a computer. A graphical user interface (GUI) is just one example of an interface, such as the windows used to store, sort, and view computer files.

Interface Designer: A person who focuses on the look and feel, such as what visual metaphors go into a graphical user interface (GUI), layout, color, and typography. They are not always responsible for the backend production.

Intranet: A closed and private system that delivers information only for members who have access to that system, typically over a secure network not accessible to outsiders.

ISP (Internet Service Provider): The party responsible for connecting a digital device to the web.

JavaScript: An object-oriented language that delivers dynamic functions.

JPEG (Joint Photographic Experts Group): A file format that was developed to handle photographs and that uses twenty-four bits of color to render millions of colors. JPEG files do not offer transparency or animation the way that GIF files do. Many JPEG formatting tools output using lossy methods where compression reduces file size. High compression will reduce the image quality, but will deliver a smaller file size. Low compression will maintain a high level of image quality, but will deliver a larger file size.

Kerning (also called Inter-Letter Spacing, Inter-Character Spacing): The space between two different typographic characters. May refer to space reduced between characters.

Leading (also called Line Spacing, Line Height): The vertical distance between lines of type, measured from one baseline to another one above or below it.

Look and Feel (also called Aesthetic, Style, Appearance): The way a website appears to match (or not match) its content, theme, or brand needs. Graphic elements such as color, image, type choice, and composition will add up to build an appropriate concept that is less about decoration and more about form and function.

Metaphor: Visuals, tasks, or actions in a user interface that help people understand how to interact with digital media. A common computing metaphor is the idea of the desktop: When we come to our computer, we see icons such as folders synonymous with how our physical desk appears.

Microblog: A type of blog with shorter entries, such as those at Twitter and Tumblr. Some microblogs feature visual media such as photographs or video. These shorter blogs may have commenting enabled for outsiders to add to the discussion.

Navigation System (also called Nav): Routes, clicks, or choices designed to move a visitor throughout a digital space.

Output: Any method used to deliver digital content from a computer to its user, such as displays, speakers, or printers.

Pattern: An element that has been arranged sequentially or repetitively in order to create a continuous design or system.

Pixel: The smallest light element rendered on a digital display. Conventional displays render 72 pixels per square inch (ppi) with others rendering 96 or 128 ppi. Higher resolutions such as Apple's Retina Display render at 326 ppi.

Pixels Per Inch (PPI): A measurement of digital resolution such as displays, scanners, and cameras. If a digital image measuring 72 × 72 pixels is printed in a 1-inch (2.5 cm) square, it would be 72 dots per inch (dpi).

PNG (Portable Network Graphics): A file format that renders millions of colors like a JPEG with the added bonus of transparency like a GIF. PNG files do not deliver animation the way an animated GIF can. Like GIF and JPEG formats, you can compress a PNG file to make it smaller.

Producer: A person who works on or oversees all aspects of electronic-media creation. They may be experts in a single design area, but they could also have a journeyman's knowledge of how each designer must contribute to the project. This can be a management position or a hands-on creative one, or both.

Prototype (also called Wireframes or Statics): A rough design that may not have interactive features, meaning buttons will not work and images will not animate, but the visual skeleton begins to appear in order to put everything in its right place.

QWERTY (pronounced *KWER-tee*): A keyboard layout that earns its name from the first six keys appearing in the top-left row, read left to right: Q-W-E-R-T-Y. Keyboard layouts change depending on language. And they can also change depending on usage, such as the DVORAK keyboard layout patented by Dr. August Dvorak, which can offer more comfort and greater typing efficiency.

Representation: A picture or model that depicts something or someone. They can be rendered using digital or printed photographs, illustrations, and icons, among other methods.

RGB (Red, Green, and Blue): An additive color system used for digital displays.

RSS (Rich Site Summary or Really Simple Syndication): A tool for collecting, publishing, sharing, and promoting frequently updated digital content such as news media or blog posts.

Scope: A statement of work that defines the problem, activities, timeline, and deliverables necessary to complete an objective or objectives.

Screen Scrape: Slang for the act of selecting, copying to the clipboard, and pasting content.

Scrolling (also Panning or Swiping): Movement through the contents of a window using an input device such as a keyboard, mouse, trackball, trackpad, or touchscreen.

SDK (Software Development Kit or Devkit): A toolset that developers use for developing software such as apps for tablets and mobile devices. They include frameworks for building applications on certain platforms, such as computer operating systems, gaming consoles, or mobile devices. Two popular mobile SDKs include Google's Android and Apple's iOS. SDKs can also be used to build smaller applications known as widgets.

Select: Pointing to an object or area, and clicking or touching it to activate it.

SEO (Search Engine Optimization): The process of improving a website's presence on search engines such as Google or Bing. Terms such as natural, organic, or algorithmic refer to optimizing a site without paying to have its search ranking promoted.

sIFR (Scalable Inman Flash Replacement): A font substitution method conceived by Shaun Inman and developed by Mike Davidson, Tomas Jogin, and Mark Wubben. It replaces a site's text type with any typeface of your choice using a combination of JavaScript, CSS, and Flash.

Simulated Sickness (also Sim Sickness): The resultant fatigue, sickness, and/or headache brought about by virtual reality experiences. Heavy head-mounted displays and poor motion tracking can induce this in some people, and at times the effects are not completely evident to the at-risk user. Not as serious as motion sickness (kinetosis), but can cause breakdowns in physical performance.

Skeuomorphic: Mimicking a person, place, or thing when designing a user interface. The calculator application is one example, where the application itself looks like a calculator. Others include designing a guitar interface with digital strings and a sound chamber for an app to play music on your smartphone or tablet.

Stereoscopic: Seeing two images of the same object viewed together to mimic depth and volume. The object must be recorded from two separate perspectives in order to achieve this effect.

Style Sheet: A document that identifies how visual elements will appear and behave.

Texture: In two-dimensional design, creating the impression that a visual rendering has a tactile quality, such as smooth, coarse, rough, or hard.

Touchpoint: The way people experience a brand, including, but not limited to, products, packaging, price, marketing, personnel, verbal communication, social media, press releases, email newsletters, blogs, music, or video.

Traditional Designer (also called Graphic Designer, Conventional Designer): Those who take on projects that use printed media as the output. It may also refer to designers who work on projects that are not digital in nature.

Typeface: Glyphs as seen by the designer, who sets text for users to read. Fonts store the data that gets rendered into the visual typeface.

URL (Uniform Resource Locator): The unique address of a digital object found on the web, and often begins with "http."

Virtual Reality (VR): Seeing and experiencing three-dimensional imagery on a digital screen, heads-up display, head-mounted display, or goggles. Can require additional equipment such as motion trackers, data gloves, and data clothing. The term is often credited to Jaron Lanier, a pioneer in early virtual reality technology and programming.

Visual Simulator: A device that delivers a motion-based experience, such as a video game. Theme park rides and flight simulators are other examples with their replication of moving imagery, turbulence, air pressure, and temperature.

Web Designer: A designer who develops websites for desktop computers, tablets such as the iPad, and smaller mobile devices such as phones.

Web-Safe Color: A limited set of colors intended to display consistently no matter the computer, browser, or operating system used.

Widget: An application with a smaller set of operations and functions that runs on top of an operating system such as Mac OS or Windows.

Wireframe (or Wire Frame, also called Box Model or Prototype): A loose, sketch-based website that shows the relationship between the visual content and the format in which it will be displayed. They are intended for reviewing preliminary designs and testing, to identify any visual problems before the full frontend gets designed. These can be interactive, built for clicking, navigating, and animating, but they can also be built in software such as Illustrator for static viewing on-screen or in print.

WUI (Web-based User Interface): A series of visual devices that come together in a web-enabled browser to deliver digital content. They can exist on televisions, desktop computers, laptops, netbooks, tablets, and mobile phones, but since each device will have a different screen size, the digital content may change.

WYSIWYG (What You See Is What You Get, pronounced *wiz-EE-wig*): Computer software that enables you to see how a design, typographic treatment, or image will appear in its final construct, whether published on paper or in pixels.

Appendixes · *Bibliography*

Chapter 1

World Wide Web Consortium; www.w3.org/

Screen: Essays on Graphic Design, New Media, and Visual Culture by Jessica Helfand
(Princeton Architectural Press, 2001)

Chapter 2

Usability Engineering
by Jakob Nielsen (Morgan Kaufmann, 1994)

Information Architects
by Richard Saul Wurman (Graphis Inc., 1997)

SWOT Analysis: Idea, Methodology, and a Practical Approach
by Nadine Pahl and Anne Richter (GRIN Verlag, 2009)

Creating the Perfect Design Brief: How to Manage Design for Strategic Advantage
by Peter L. Phillips (Allworth Press, 2004)

Information Architecture for the World Wide Web
by Louis Rosenfeld and Peter Morville (O'Reilly Media, 2006)

"Managing the Development of Large Software Systems"
by Winston Royce, available online at www.cs.umd.edu/
class/spring2003/cmsc838p/Process/waterfall.pdf

Managing the Design Process – Implementing Design: An Essential Manual for the Working Designer
by Terry Lee Stone (Rockport Publishers, 2010)

Chapter 3

Mac OS X Developer Library; http://developer.apple.com/
library/mac/navigation/

Designing Web Navigation
by James Kalbach (O'Reilly Media, 2007)

Creating a Website: The Missing Manual
by Matthew MacDonald (O'Reilly Media, 2011)

Chapter 4

World Wide Web Consortium; dev.w3.org/

"Web Design Is 95% Typography"; www.informationarchi-tects.jp/en/the-web-is-all-about-typography-period/

"Reactions to 95% Typography"; www.informationarchitects.
jp/en/webdesign-is-95-typography-partii

Typographic Design: Form and Communication
by Rob Carter, Ben Day, and Philip Meggs (Wiley, 2002)

Typography Workbook
by Timothy Samara (Rockport Publishers, 2006)

Design Elements: A Graphic Style Manual
by Timothy Samara (Rockport Publishers, 2007)

Chapter 5

Graphic Design Processes: Universal to Unique
by Ken Hiebert (Thomson Learning, 1991)

Layout: The Design of the Printed Page
by Allen Hurlburt (Watson-Guptill Publications, 1977)

"Death of the Websafe Color Palette?"
by David Lehn and Hadley Stern; www.physics.ohio-state.
edu/~wilkins/color/websafecolors.html

Digital Media: An Introduction
by Richard L. Lewis and James Luciana (Prentice Hall, 2004)

Design Fundamentals
by Robert G. Scott (McGraw-Hill, 1951)

Chapter 6

Augmented reality; www.se.rit.edu/~jrv/research/ar/

3D technologies; http://web.mit.edu/newsoffice/2011/
glasses-free-3d-0504.html

AR technologies; www.artoolworks.com/ and www.hitl.
washington.edu/artoolkit/

The Metaphysics of Virtual Reality
by Michael Heim (Oxford University Press, 1994)

"The Visionary: A digital pioneer questions what technology has wrought" by Jennifer Kahn
(The New Yorker, July 11 & 18, 2011)

Understanding Comics by Scott McCloud (Tundra Pub, 1993)

Type and Image: The Language of Graphic Design
by Phillp B. Meggs (Wiley, 1992)

Cuts: texts 1959–2004
by Carl André and James Sampson Meyer

Chapter 7

Gap reverts; http://money.cnn.com/2010/10/08/news/
companies/gap_logo/index.htm

Handbook of Communication: Models, Perspectives, Strategies by Uma Narula
(Atlantic Publishers & Distributors, 2006)

Fast Food Nation: The Dark Side of the All-American Meal
by Eric Schlosser (Harper Perennial, 2005)

Managing the Design Process – Concept Development: An Essential Manual for the Working Designer
by Terry Lee Stone (Rockport Publishers, 2010)

Resources

Browsers, Formats, and Sizes
https://browserlab.adobe.com
http://browsersize.googlelabs.com

Typography
http://alistapart.com
http://blog.typekit.com
http://css-tricks.com/what-beautiful-html-code-looks-like/
http://maxbruinsma.nl/deepsites/typography.html
www.emigre.com
www.fonts.com
www.mikeindustries.com/blog/sifr
www.typography.com
www.w3.org/TR/css3-fonts/

AIGA Design Business and Ethics
www.aiga.org/design-business-and-ethics/

Icograda Online Document Library
www.icograda.org/resources/library.htm

3D TVs: Frequently Asked Questions
www.consumerreports.org/cro/electronics-computers/tvs-services/hdtv/3d-tvs/3d-tv-faq/index.htm, January 2011

Backgrounds and Images
http://patterntap.com/tap/collection/backgrounds

Color and Color Systems
http://kuler.adobe.com/

The Fold in Retrospect
http://blog.clicktale.com/2006/12/23/unfolding-the-fold/

Responsive Web Design
www.alistapart.com/articles/responsive-web-design
www.aiga.org/responsive-web-design-resources-and-recap/

Design Methodologies
http://agilemanifesto.org/

2Creatives
www.2creatives.com

Acqualia
http://acqualia.com

Archrival
720 O Street
Lincoln, NE 68508
U.S.A.
http://archrival.com

Big Spaceship, LLC
45 Main Street, Suite 716
Brooklyn, NY 11201
U.S.A.
http://bigspaceship.com

Mandy Brown
http://aworkinglibrary.com

Neil Brown
http://nomadicbydesign.com/neil

carbonhouse, Inc.
http://carbonhouse.com

Dutch Icon
Maashaven z.z. 2
3081 AE Rotterdam
The Netherlands
http://dutchicon.com

The Dye Lab
http://thedyelab.com

Matt Fangman
Fangman Design
P.O. Box 2184
Austin, TX 78768
U.S.A.
http://fangmandesign.com

Firebelly Design
2701 W. Thomas Street, 2nd Floor
Chicago, IL 60622
U.S.A.
http://firebellydesign.com

GOOD
915 N. Citrus Avenue
Los Angeles, CA 90038
U.S.A.
http://good.is

Christian Helms
Helms Workshop
2415 E. 8th Street
Austin, TX 78704
U.S.A.
info@helmsworkshop.com
http://helmsworkshop.com

Jessica Hische
http://jessicahische.is/awesome

Instrument
http://weareinstrument.com

Landers Miller Design
146 W. 29th Street, Suite 6RE-1
New York, NY 10001
U.S.A.
http://landersmiller.com

Lifeislottery
http://lifeislottery.com

Joshua Mauldin
http://joshuamauldin.com

Method
972 Mission Street, Floor 2
San Francisco, CA 94103
U.S.A.
http://method.com

MODE
1307 W. Morehead Street
Suite 102
Charlotte, NC 28208
U.S.A.
http://madebymode.com

Belmer Negrillo
Mindness.net
http://mindness.net/ixd

Gopal Raju
Convax Solutions
http://convax.com

Jason Santa Maria
http://jasonsantamaria.com

Benjamin K. Shown
723 Federal Avenue E., Apt. 2
Seattle, WA 98102
U.S.A.
http://benjamink.com

Silverpoint
3600 Clipper Mill Road, Suite 422
Baltimore, MD 21211
U.S.A.
http://silverpoint.net

SlideRoom
12001 N. Central Expy.
Suite #1120
Dallas, TX 75243
U.S.A.
http://slideroom.com

smashLAB
1205 - 207 W. Hastings Street
Vancouver, British Columbia
V6B 1H7 Canada
http://smashlab.com

Social Design House
201 E. Main Street, #207
Rock Hill, SC 29730
U.S.A.
http://socialdesignhouse.com

Paul Soulellis
Soulellis Studio, Inc.
http://soulellis.com

Sparkbox
411 E. 5th Street
Dayton, OH 45402
U.S.A.
http://seesparkbox.com

Spunk Design Machine
4933 34th Avenue South
Minneapolis, MN 55417
U.S.A.
http://spkdm.com

Studiobanks
421 Penman Street, Suite 310
Charlotte, NC 28203
U.S.A.
http://studiobanks.com

Rafael Stüken
Büro für Grafik Design
Annastraße 55
Cologne 50968
Germany
http://raffaelstueken.de

Tripleships, Inc.
4F Noguchi Bldg.
Aobadai, Meguro-ku
Tokyo 153-0042
Japan
http://tripleships.com

Twofold Creative
1/451 Sherwood Road
Sherwood Q
Brisbane, Queensland 4075
Australia
admin@twofoldcreative.com

Ultranoir
26, rue de Charonne
Paris 75011
France
http://ultranoir.com

UnderConsideration
http://underconsideration.com

version industries (v)
68 Jay Street
Brooklyn, NY 11201
U.S.A.
http://versionindustries.com

Voice
217 Gilbert Street
Adelaide SA 5000
Australia
http://voicedesign.net

X